MW00364360

A Thousand Years of Hebrew History
PSALMS

A Thousand Years of Hebrew History
PSALMS
Laud O. Vaught

Pathway
PRESS

Book Editor: Wanda Griffith
Editorial Assistant: Tammy Hatfield
Copy Editors: Esther Metaxas
Cresta Shawver
Inside Layout: Mark Shuler

Library of Congress Card Catalog Number: 00-100088

ISBN: 0-87148-944-9

Dedication

To my wife, *Jewell,*
and my children—*Melinda, Laud,*
Denice, Dwight—
who together have become the
five additional "Hallelujah Psalms" in my life.

Contents

FOREWORD

Whether you are a longtime devotee of the Psalms or a beginner wanting to learn about the Psalms, you will want to read *Psalms: A Thousand Years of Hebrew History*. Once you begin to read it, you will not want to put it down. Having read it, it will become a permanent reference work on the Psalms, to which you will return again and again for information, practical knowledge and inspiration.

Understandable, yet profound in depth and broad in scope, *Psalms: A Thousand Years of Hebrew History* is a treasure of insight on the Psalms that appeals not only to the devotional reader but also to the seasoned theologian. This book is a vast resource on the Psalms for preachers, teachers and students. It is concise and orderly in its presentation, encyclopedic in its content, and practical in its application.

For more than 46 years, Dr. Laud O. Vaught has been an ordained minister in the Church of God. He has devoted his life to Christian education as teacher and president at Northwest Bible College and as professor and administrator at Lee University. From that large reservoir of scholarship and experience, he has written a book on the Psalms that is not merely good, but truly excellent and unique.

Dr. Vaught has rightly called the Psalms "a thousand years of Hebrew history." The Psalms are not merely songs—they are hymns, prayers, spiritual songs, and recitations that celebrate, interpret, and commemorate the historical experiences of Israel and individual Israelites in relationship with God.

Dr. Vaught's treatment of the Psalms will prove to be equally valuable, whether it be used as a textbook in college, university or seminary classrooms, or as a study guide in Sunday school classes, Bible study groups or personal devotion.

The character of the author of this book is, in large measure, that which will make the reading and study of this book on Psalms a spiritually enriching experience. Dr. Vaught, a devoted husband, father and grandfather, has been a spiritual mentor to hundreds of ministers. He is an outstanding Christian who has proven his integrity and commitment to Christ over many decades. His doctrinal and practical perspectives on the Psalms are, appropriately, reflections of his own lofty values and his long personal journey of faith in communion with Christ and his fellow Christians.

—Daniel L. Black, Th.D., Editor-Writer
Adult Sunday School Literature
Pathway Press, Cleveland, Tennessee

PREFACE

This work was prepared in its original form for presentation to a class of pastors, graduate students and other Christian workers at the Han Young Theological University in Seoul, South Korea. Since its presentation many have encouraged me to make the material available to a wider audience for use in the classroom, as supplemental Sunday school material, external study text, as well as personal devotional resource.

The Bibliography is limited to those texts in my private library which I have used in more than 40 years of study and research. Many other titles can be researched from the libraries of Schools of Religion. Scripture references have been placed in the body of the text to make them more accessible. The Scripture quotations are from the *New International Version* and the *New American Standard Bible.*

Endnotes have been chosen in order to simplify the process. Only those items which cannot be readily found in most reference books have been noted.

Acknowledgments

Thanks to Melinda Vaught Norton, who encouraged me to prepare this manuscript and was an inestimable aid in its preparation. Also thanks to her daughter, Sarah, for her technical assistance with the computer.

1

Uniqueness of the Book of Psalms

The Book of Psalms is unique in the Old Testament and, indeed, in the whole Bible. With 150 divisions, it is the longest book in the entire Bible. Historically, the time period is the longest of any other book. In fact, the material in the Psalms covers a time period representing virtually that of the entire Old Testament. In terms of authorship, no other book in Scripture represents the writing of so many individuals. It is also unique in Scripture in that it contains both the longest (Psalm 119) and the shortest (Psalm 117) chapter in both the Old or New Testaments.

As to its location, it is central to the entire Bible in as much as Psalm 118:8 is the middle verse in the Word. No other book in the entire Bible has five distinct books within a book. More will be said about these unique qualities later.

Time Element in Psalms

We have already noted that Psalms covers a time span roughly equal to that of the Old Testament. The oldest psalm is Psalm 90, which was written by Moses, who also wrote the first five books of the Bible—the Pentateuch. In the providence of God, Moses had been "taken out" (which is the meaning of the name Moses) of the water and became an adopted child of Pharaoh's daughter. In this capacity, he received the best schooling available, because Egypt was a center of learning.

The Pentateuch could not have been written before the wilderness wanderings of 40 years that followed the deliverance of the children of Israel from Egypt. The 120 years of Moses' life is divided into three 40-year periods. The first 40 years were in Egypt, but the material in the first five books had not yet occurred. In the second 40-year period, he lived on the backside of the desert in the land of Midian. There is no evidence of a revelation from God until the end of that period, when God appeared to him in a burning bush. The last 40 years were spent after he crossed the Red Sea. It is not until after the Sinai experience that Moses would have had the time or the revelation necessary to write the five books of the Pentateuch.

I believe that Psalm 90 was written early in the period. It is titled "A Prayer of Moses the Man of God," and the internal evidence gives us a hint of his age, which places the psalm during the Sinai stay or shortly after.

The length of our days
is seventy years—or eighty,
if we have the strength (90:10).

These are not the words of a man of 90 or 120. Moses would have been about 80 or perhaps 81 years old at Sinai. If the psalm was not written at that time, it would have been shortly after. From this internal evidence, it is likely that Psalm 90 was the first of his writings.

Now concerning the close of Psalms. We know that Psalm 137 was written during the Babylonian Captivity (see vv. 4, 5, 8). This psalm would have been later than 586 B.C., which was the date of the destruction of Jerusalem. Psalms 120—134 are believed to have been written after the return from captivity. The second Temple was built in 515 B.C. This is especially borne out in the following passage:

> *When the Lord brought back*
> *the captives to Zion,*
> *we were like men who dreamed* (126:1).

We have no difficulty then in determining a time span of about 1500 B.C. to about 500 B.C. Some think the closing psalm to be even later, but the 1,000-year span can be determined by internal evidence.

Title of the Book

We are accustomed to seeing the title as simply Psalms or the Psalms of David. The truth is that the latter is somewhat misleading because slightly fewer than half the Psalms are titled by or for David (see "Authorship"). We do not know how many of the untitled Psalms (sometimes called "Orphan Psalms") belong to David.

We do know, for example, that Psalm 2, which is untitled, is attributed to David in the New Testament (Acts 4:25). In the same manner, we do not know with assurance whether those that bear his name were written by him, because the same preposition is used in Hebrew—whether it is "by David," in the sense of being written by

David, or "for David," in the sense of being written at David's request, or "to David," in the sense of being dedicated to him. The Hebrew language of that day simply did not make that distinction.

We must also deal with the "Orphan Psalms," many of which may have belonged to David. We have already seen that Psalm 2 is ascribed to him in Acts 4:25, although it is untitled in the Psalms. It is also possible that a psalm may have been written by David and discovered long after his death, so that the scribe would be uncertain of its origin. Some scholars believe that longer psalms were sometimes divided and the second half remained untitled, as appears to be true in Psalms 42 and 43, which are titled to the sons of Korah. But we will see more about this later.

The Greek title was simply Psalmoi, meaning "songs which were accompanied by stringed instruments." This was supplied by the Septuagint, the Greek translation from the Hebrew made about 250 B.C. Many English Bibles still use the word Psalter, which was made a household word by Martin Luther through his German translation.

According to H.C. Leupold[1], the Hebrew title for the Psalms is sepher tehillim, which is translated "Book of Praise—Psalms." That would seem to indicate that all Psalms were songs of praise, which is not altogether accurate, although the later portion of the book is given almost exclusively to that form.

Authorship of Psalms

We have already established that the book was written over a period of approximately 1,000 years. This would rule out the idea of a single author.

We should start with the idea that the book was first an attempt to collect the psalms of David. At the same time, it will make our study easier if we begin with the concept that a book covering 1,000 years might be a compilation, rather than a single book.

The final editor of Psalms makes this clear by dividing the work into five different books. Although these divisions are not a part of the inspired writing, they certainly add a great deal to our understanding.

There are five distinct books identified in Psalms:

Book I Psalms 1-41
Book II Psalms 42-72
Book III Psalms 73-89
Book IV Psalms 90-106
Book V Psalms 107-150

The collector of Book I clearly intended to bring together the psalms of David, because each of these psalms bears his name (with the exception of those which may have been divided and Psalm 2, which we established as Davidic based on Acts 4:25). This leaves only Psalm 1, which was probably not Davidic, but written as an introduction to the entire five books by the final collector.

Book II was plainly intended to be attributed to David, because at the close of Book II we find the words in 72:20, "This concludes the prayers [prayers and psalms were often used interchangeably in the Hebrew] of David son of Jesse." This might seem to be strange, considering that Book II begins with the psalms of the sons of Korah. It will help us then to turn to 1 Chronicles 6 and read: "These are the men David put in charge of the music" (v. 31), and "Here are the men who served, together with their sons . . . " (v. 33), "the son of Korah" (v. 37), and "Heman's associate Asaph" (v. 39).

It may be assumed that the prayers of David included those who had been appointed by David, since Asaph is also found in this section. The Hebrews, who knew the history of David's musical team, would have no trouble with this.

With some reasonable assumption then, we could place Book I as the first attempt to gather David's writings. Since they are in a separate book, it is quite likely that some time elapsed before more of David's work was found. At some point the decision was made to include the work done by David's appointees with the manuscripts of David and prepare Book II. More will be said about this when we look at the individual psalms.

Book III contains Psalms 73-89 and are mainly written by Asaph. Only Psalm 86 is ascribed to David. Here again, this psalm may have been discovered after Book II was completed and was used in scroll form for years. It will be helpful to understand that these psalms were handwritten (most likely on separate pieces of material) and could have been easily scattered in the normal process of use.

Book IV begins with the majestic prayer of Moses that we know as Psalm 90. Since Psalms 91 through 100 are untitled, I am inclined to embrace the rabbinic tradition, which holds that Psalms 90-100 are of Mosaic authorship. The nature of the literature may add some credence to the theory that Psalm 101 and 103 are works of David in Book IV. I do not dispute the thought that the content of Psalm 102 resembles the other two and may have indeed been a part of 101 originally. Also, some may not have been titled until they were included in a scroll for permanent record and distribution. By that time the scribe might have been uncertain about its authorship and therefore left it untitled.

That would add credibility to the theory that many untitled psalms were written by David.

Book V contains 44 psalms, many of which are Davidic. Others, by their very content, are obviously post-Davidic. These would include the Songs of Ascent to be sung going up to the Temple—which had not yet been built in David's lifetime—and the lament over the destruction of that same Temple hundreds of years later.

In terms of authorship of all the Psalms, David was the primary writer with the greatest number attributed to him. He is followed by Asaph and then by the sons of Korah. Solomon is regarded as the author of two, while Moses has one ascribed to him, but may have indeed written the first 11 of Book IV. Heman, who was known for his wisdom during Solomon's reign (1 Kings 4:31), is assigned authorship of Psalm 88. Ethan, a descendant of Judah (1 Chronicles 2:6), is credited with Psalm 89.

The remaining question is, Was there an unnamed writer who wrote Psalm 1 as an introduction to the collection, organized the books as they appear in the Septuagint and perhaps wrote at least some of the final untitled psalms? I believe so.

The book could not have been closed before the time of Ezra and Nehemiah because the Babylonian Captivity is described in Psalm 137 and the last five psalms that will be discussed later. These five psalms, according to F. Delitzsch[2], resemble the language of the liturgical Bercha of the second Temple. This means they would have been written well after the second Temple was in use, near the time of the Persian supremacy (465–425 B.C.). If this is accurate, it places these last psalms in the time of Ezra and Nehemiah.

We know that 13 years after Nehemiah came to Jerusalem and repaired the walls (455 B.C.), Ezra took the lead in a religious reform that included reading the Law of Moses to the people and encouraging the renewal of Temple worship (see Nehemiah 8). While Nehemiah was governor, Ezra was the priest who was well-versed in both history and literature. It is not unthinkable that he may have been the final editor and used what became the Hymn Book of Israel as part of the spiritual reform strategy.

If there is indeed a connection between the liturgical Bercha of the second Temple, as Delitzsch suggests, it is not unthinkable that Ezra may well have used the completion of this hymnbook to help restore the deteriorating spiritual condition of Israel.

The Nature of Hebrew Poetry

Forget that it does not sound like the poetry you learned in school. The Hebrew of the Old Testament is a language 3,000 years old, and we can expect it to be a little different. We were taught to rhyme the sound at the end of a line or within the line.

Hebrew poetry does not have a rhyme of sound, and it is good for us that it does not. If it did, it could not be translated because the sound is different and we could not change it to Greek or English and have the same sound and meaning.

Hebrew poetry rhymes in thought rather than sound. If a person wrote a thought and then on the next line wrote the same thought in different words, that was poetry. If someone wrote a thought and then on the next line wrote something directly opposite to the first thought, that too was poetry. But there were also other options. The first line could contain a thought and the second line could be a progression of that thought. Just as in our rhyme of sound, it made the poem easier to remember.

Types of Hebrew Poetry

We are indebted to Bishop Lowth[3] for the terminology that helps identify the types and usage of Hebrew poetry. Parallelism is the primary term used by Bishop Lowth. Variations based on this term include the following: synonymous, antithetical, amplification and response. We will look at each of these separately and point out examples of each type from Scripture. You may sometimes find these types used by others under different names. However, these four will bring understanding to the basic nature of Hebrew poetry.

1. *Synonymous Parallelism.* This is the basic type in which one line is followed by another of the same meaning but in different words. An early example of this type of expression is found in Genesis 1:27, where we are told:

So God created man in his own image,
in the image of God he created him.

Here we see one statement in two word combinations that mean the same thing.

We find this type of combination throughout the Old Testament, but we will only look at the more familiar ones from Psalms. Note Psalm 19:1, 2:

The heavens declare the glory of God;
the skies proclaim the work of his hands.
Day after day they pour forth speech;
night after night they display knowledge.

Note how carefully and beautifully these expressions flow together. No wonder so many learn Psalm 19 at an early age.

Again in Psalm 24:1 a favorite passage forms a synonymous parallel:

The earth is the Lord's, and everything in it,
the world, and all who live in it.

Note also Psalm 33:6:

By the word of the Lord
were the heavens made,
their starry hosts by the breath of his mouth.

These samples demonstrate the concept of the synonymous parallel—repeating line one but in different phraseology. Reading the Psalms would not be interesting if they were all synonymous parallels. Let us look now at what might be called the reverse parallel.

2. *Antithetical Parallelism.* Here we find the exact opposite of the one that we just reviewed. A statement is made and an opposite appears on the next line. Both statements will be true. There is no contradiction because they deal with a truth, which is not the same truth spoken at first. A few examples will help clarify what is meant by antithetical parallelism:

They are brought to their knees and fall,
but we rise up and stand firm (20:8).

For the Lord watches over
the way of the righteous,
but the way of the wicked will perish (1:6).

Note the antithesis of this combination. Psalm 15:4 describes the man who will dwell in God's holy hill:

Who despises a vile man
but honors those who fear the Lord. . . .

It is important to know that Hebrew poetry is not confined to Psalms. It is used throughout the Old Testament in the Historical and Prophetic as well as the Poetic Books.

Your gates will always stand open,
they will never be shut,
day or night (Isaiah 60:11).

Perhaps the most dramatic use of this form is Ecclesiastes 3:1-9:

There is a time for everything,
and a season for every activity under heaven:
a time to be born and a time to die,
a time to plant and a time to uproot.
a time to kill and a time to heal,
a time to tear down and a time to build,
a time to weep and a time to laugh (vv. 1-4).

Perhaps no more powerful review of the plight of man has ever been written. Let us now look at what we might call a combination of these two concepts.

3. *Amplification.* In this concept, we see the second line adding to the meaning of the first. Many use the term *progression* to describe this form. Note Psalm 18:14:

He shot his arrows
and scattered the enemies,

great bolts of lightning
and routed them.

Here the writer says the same thing, but the second line explains the first. The "arrows" of God were in the first line, but explained in the second line. How could we know what the arrows were if they were not explained in the line which follows? The psalmist also uses the idea of progression in his poetry in order to make it more meaningful, as in Psalm 129:3:

Ploughmen have plowed my back
and made their furrows long.

In Psalm 132:12 the second line is a promise based upon the observance of the first:

If your sons keep my covenant
and the statutes I teach them,
then their sons will sit on your throne
for ever and ever.

As we move to the fourth major type, remember that Hebrew poetry is the most ancient form known to human literature (Adam Clarke[4]). If it sometimes seems to follow its own rules, that is because there were no rules of poetry existing when these passages were written.

4. *Response.* Remember that the further we go from the synonymous parallel, the more variation we find. There is something much like this in English poetry when we leave the basic rules and move into free verse.

He blessed them,
and their numbers greatly increased,
and he did not let their herds diminish (107:38).

Psalm 1 provides us with an often-used description of the righteous man where this concept is used:

He is like a tree planted by streams of water,
which yields its fruit in season
and whose leaf does not wither.
Whatever he does prospers (v. 3).

A prayer of David in Psalm 5 also provides a good example that moves almost into prose while retaining the poetical rhythm:

In the morning, O Lord,
you hear my voice;
in the morning
I lay my requests before you
and wait in expectation (v. 3).

Perhaps in Psalm 19 we could draw one last example concerning the law of the Lord:

The law of the Lord is perfect,
reviving the soul.
The statutes of the Lord are trustworthy,
making wise the simple (v. 7).

There are many different variations, but these four types demonstrate the pattern of the earliest-known poetry, not only in the Bible but also in other literature.

2

Acrostic and Didactic Psalms

The word *acrostic* should be familiar because we use its principle quite often. We teach by placing the letters of the word down the side of the chalkboard and then make other words or statements out of each letter used in the original word. It can be expanded in many ways.

For example, sometimes we use the word *Christian* and then follow it with *Christ—without Him I Am Nothing*. The *i, a, n* then become an acrostic. The same thing happens when we place the name *CHRIST* on our board or paper. We may place it vertically and then add the following:

C hildren need Him.
Homes need Him.
R ejoice because God has come.
I nciting others to know Him.
S owing His love in the world.
T rusting Him for our salvation.

The use of acrostics helps us remember certain words or truths.

The Hebrews, in a basic approach to acrostics, concentrated on their alphabet of 22 letters. Thus, each letter formed the framework of the entire psalm. Our first readers did the same thing when we read:

A is for apple so round and so red.

B is for boy so early to bed.

C is for children learning to read. . . .

Some of the psalms are constructed so that the first letter of the Hebrew alphabet begins the first line and the second letter the second line, until all 22 consecutive letters of the alphabet have been used. Obviously these constructions are obliterated in any translation.

When we talked about the *parallel concept* of Hebrew poetry, we stated that we were fortunate that translations did not obscure its meaning. In the acrostic we have no idea that it is there unless we see it in the original Hebrew. Even with my limited knowledge of the Old Testament language, it becomes obvious as soon as I see the form on the right side of the page where each line begins.

Psalm 119

Without doubt this is the queen of all alphabetical psalms. It contains the type of acrostic we have discussed with 22 stanzas. We identify the 22 because they follow specifically the Hebrew alphabet. Each of the eight verses in the stanza, or *strophe*, begins with the same letter. Most Bible versions will show those divisions with the Hebrew letter used. Some also supply the name of the alphabetical letters as well as the character itself. The names are listed for each of the 22 sections as follows:

verses 1-8	Aleph
verses 9-16	Beth

verses 17-24	Gimel
verses 25-32	Daleth
verses 33-40	He
verses 41-48	Waw (*Vav*)
verses 49-56	Zayin (*Zain*)
verses 57-64	Heth (*Cheth*)
verses 65-72	Teth
verses 73-80	Yodh (*Yod*)
verses 81-88	Kaph (*Caph*)
verses 89-96	Lamedh (*Lamed*)
verses 97-104	Mem
verses 105-112	Nun
verses 113-120	Samekh (*Samech*)
verses 121-128	Ayin (*Ain*)
verses 129-136	Pe (*Phe*)
verses 137-144	Tsadhe (*Tzaddi*)
verses 145-152	Qoph (*Koph*)
verses 153-160	Resh
verses 161-168	Sin (*Shin*)
verses 169-176	Taw (*Tau*)

The words in parentheses are alternate pronunciations that still exist in some translations. Some letters were pronounced differently in the Hebrew even as they may be in the English or other languages.

In Psalm 119, the longest chapter in the Bible, each verse extols the Word of God. We now look further at the theme of this masterful literary work.

It may appear at first glance that it was written by an old Jewish professor who wanted to impress his students. We are indebted to Delitzsch[1] for an insight far stranger than we might imagine. Verse 9 suggests that the writer is a young man when he asks the question, "How can a young man keep his way pure?" This is answered in verses 99 and 100: "I have more insight than all my teachers, for I meditate on your statutes. I have more understanding than the elders, for I obey your precepts."

This not only established his youth, but it also verified that he either lived in a time when the elders had forsaken the Word of God, or he was in a country that had no knowledge of God. The writer cited believes the latter.

Further, we see this young man living where the government was hostile to the Word. "Though rulers sit together and slander me, your servant will meditate on your decrees" (v. 23). Note also verse 161: "Rulers persecute me without cause, but my heart trembles at your word." The setting does not appear to be in Judah or Israel, but in a land hostile to Jewish religious views.

Note also in verse 61, "Though the wicked bind me with ropes, I will not forget your law." This picture is continued in verse 84 with the question, "How long must your servant wait? When will you punish my persecutors?" Is he indeed bound in prison by those who hate the law of God? The answer seems to be yes.

Verse 109 even suggests that death may be the result of his loyalty to the law of God: "Though I constantly take my life in my hands, I will not forget your law." This idea is strengthened by verse 107: "I have suffered much; preserve my life, O Lord, according to your word."

This idea is further strengthened by verse 112: "My heart is set on keeping your decrees to the very end." These verses suggest a young man in prison in a foreign land who may be expecting to die for his loyalty to the law of God.

Further, the concept of the author's imprisonment may explain why he would spend his days in developing such a complex piece of literature. He is extolling the law of God, for which he is being persecuted. This endeavor allows him to meditate day and night upon God's law as Psalm 1 exhorts.

Let us look now at the themes upon which these strophes are built. All, of course, are related to the Word of God. But is this the only theme? What is the message of each concerning the Word? An interesting way to study is to go through the 22 divisions and make a single statement of how the Word is affecting this author. The following is a suggestion:

- Aleph—In praise of fidelity to the Word
- Beth—The keeping of the Word is the virtue of all virtues.
- Gimel—Prayer for the grace of enlightenment through the Word
- Daleth—Strength through the Word
- He—Preservation through the Word
- Waw—Joyful confession through the Word
- Zayin—God's Word is all his thought and pursuit.
- Heth—He cleaves to those who fear God.
- Teth—The salutary element of his humbling through the Word
- Yodh—He is in need of comfort from the Word.
- Kaph—The sigh of "how long" until God's Word triumphs
- Lamedh—Without the Word of God, he would despair.
- Mem—The Word is his wisdom in difficult circumstance.

- Nun—He has maintained his fidelity to the Word even during his persecution.
- Samekh—He abhors the apostates.
- Ayin—He is oppressed, but God will not allow him to be crushed.
- Pe—The ungodly will not prevail over him.
- Tsadhe—The prevailing godlessness about him is consuming his zeal.
- Qoph—His desire that God would hear his cry
- Resh—His desire that God's helpful pity would revive him
- Sin—He clings fast to God though persecuted by princes.
- Taw—He is an isolated and imperiled sheep.

The plaintive cry of the one in need is clearly seen in the last two verses (vv. 175, 176):

Let me live that I may praise you,
and may your laws sustain me.
I have strayed like a lost sheep.
Seek your servant,
for I have not forgotten your commands.

Psalms 111, 112

We have both Leupold[2] and Delitzsch[3] to thank for calling our attention to a very special relationship between these two psalms. Many modern commentators simply say they are both acrostic or they say nothing at all. These authors describe both the acrostic nature and other relationships that exist between the two.

A close study looks at these two psalms together. When we first read that these are both acrostics built on the

Hebrew alphabet, we naturally look for 22 divisions as we saw in Psalm 119. When we find that each has 10 verses, so that together they only total 20 verses, we ask how this can be. Some might think that a mistake had been made in the classification. But the two authors above both demonstrate the unusual relationship.

Looking at the two together, we find that in each there are eight verses consisting of 22 lines:

- Verses 1 and 2 contain the first two letters in the Hebrew alphabet—Aleph and Beth.
- Verse 2—Gimel and Daleth
- Verse 3—He and Waw
- Verse 4—Zayin and Heth
- Verse 5—Teth and Yodh
- Verse 6—Kaph and Lamedh
- Verse 7—Mem and Nun
- Verse 8—Samekh and Ayin
- Verse 9—Pe, Tsadhe, and Qoph
- Verse 10—Resh, Sin and Taw.

We see immediately that each verse consists of two lines until we reach verses 9 and 10. Each of these contains three lines, completing the 22 we would expect to find.

A closer examination reveals that the two psalms are twins, not only in form but also in content. It may be said that Psalm 111 praises the government of God, while Psalm 112 praises those whose conduct is patterned after the divine qualities previously described.

Without including endless detail, we will make a comparison or two to help understand what the author intended in the twin psalms. In Psalm 111:3, the psalmist speaking of

God says: "Glorious and majestic are his deeds, and his righteousness endures forever." The parallel verse in Psalm 112 says of man: "Wealth and riches are in his house, and his righteousness endures forever." An interesting study would be to continue comparing parallel descriptions about God in 111 and the parallel statements in the same verse in 112. Note especially the parallels used in verses 4 and 8 of each, and the skillful use of an antithetical parallel in verse 10.

No hint is given as to the authorship. Some have suggested that it was in the time of Haggai and Zechariah, because riches seem to have been "in the house" rather than on the farm—that is, the post-agricultural period. But this still doesn't identify the author.

Nature of the Acrostics in Psalms 24, 25

We deal with these psalms together because they have the same irregular structure. That is, they depart from the consistent alphabetical order to variations that have similarities. Both are titled with Davidic authorship. Since the departure occurs in both, we must consider it a deliberate departure rather than an error in trying to follow the system. It is difficult to explain why they generally follow the Hebrew alphabet, but not perfectly. Leupold[4] points out that in both psalms the *Waw* strophe is omitted. There is no reason offered for this departure, although it occurs in both psalms. Both psalms have a second *Pe* at the close that must again be deliberate, but there is no explanation as to what the author intended by the change.

This departure is not unusual because poetry has never been a fixed entity. In English grammar, we learn the rules and then we learn the departure from the rules. For this reason, we considered Psalm 119 first. In this psalm, the rules are followed exactly and form a base for the departures we find later.

It would be interesting, however, to know why the same author deliberately changed the alphabetical structure in two psalms in exactly the same way.

Psalm 37

Psalm 37 deals with the problem of evildoers. It is an acrostic form with two verses dedicated to each letter of the Hebrew alphabet. To be more specific, verse 1 begins with the first letter, Aleph, and verse 3 begins with the second letter, Beth, and so on. The writing between these pairs does not need to conform to the previous line. For some reason, yet undetermined, the Ayin is omitted. Daleth is assigned only one verse in the *New International Version*, as is Kaph. This accounts for the 40 verses rather than the 44 as would have been expected with two verses for each of 22 letters.

Psalm 145

This psalm is the last of those known as acrostics. It is a hymn of praise, which celebrates God's care for all His creatures. Delitzsch[5] tells us that it was the ancient church's psalm for the noonday repast. It was also used by some at Holy Communion.

The psalm is *distichous* (arranged in pairs), but the distich Nun is missing. Many have tried to explain the missing part, but because of the volume of material, it is too large to be of much value to us.

A good exercise would be to read aloud the words of this psalm privately and drink in its beauty as a hymn of praise to a bountiful King.

DIDACTIC PSALMS

Didactic psalms are those which are designed to teach. It is true that many psalms contain teaching elements, but teaching is the main purpose of the didactic psalm.

Psalm 1

In the last chapter, I mentioned that Psalm 1 was written as an introductory psalm. Now I will explain why. The Book of Psalms teaches that there are only two types of persons—the godly and the ungodly. This is the theme of Psalm 1, which serves as an introduction to the entire book and repeats this truth many times.

In present-day theology, we divide good men and bad men into many categories:

- Good men who do bad things and bad men who do good things
- Good men who are sick and must do bad things, because they cannot do good things
- Bad men who are good, because they try to do good and yet past experiences prevent them. We even hear that there are no such things as bad men. There are only men who do bad things.

Psalm 1 makes it clear that this teaching is confusing. Men are godly or they are ungodly. Verses 1-3 describe the godly and verses 4-6 describe the ungodly. There is no middle ground. The exposition on these two subjects in Psalm 1 follows:

Blessed is the man who does not walk
in the counsel of the wicked

or stand in the way of sinners,
or sit in the seat of the mockers.

The godly man must separate himself from evil in order to live godly. It is impossible to follow the path and do the things ascribed to godly men until the evil ways are forsaken. The writer does not say that forsaking evil makes us godly. That is an erroneous teaching that has caused many to fail. Having forsaken the way of the world, the godly now does what the ungodly cannot do:

But his delight is in
the law of the Lord,
And on his law he meditates
day and night . . . (v. 2).

Remember that when this was written, the law was the Torah, the first five books of the Old Testament. Yet, some find no value in the Old Testament! Verse 3 describes the blessings of the godly:

He is like a tree
planted by streams of water . . .

A planted tree is not just any tree in the forest. It is chosen and placed where the owner planned it. Note that the streams are plural. If one area of supply dries up, God always has a source of supply for the godly from another direction.

Which yields its fruit in season . . .

Each of us has a season of bearing fruit. Every Christian has fruit—and remember that it is not for the tree, but for those who pass by. If we miss that season, it cannot be restored.

And whose leaf does not wither. . . .

This has nothing to do with wrinkles. The leaf is the chlorophyll of the soul, which absorbs the Sonlight that is necessary for fruit. I have seen 80-year-old people with the Sonlight shining from the soul. I have also seen 18-year-olds whose lives have withered.

Whatever he does prospers.

Some have tried to change this line, but to the godly, it is a promise fulfilled because the godly follows His direction. God always blesses the work He has chosen for us if we find and follow it.

The last part of this psalm stands in stark contrast to the first because the godly and the wicked have little in common. Note verses 4-6:

Not so the wicked!
They are like chaff
that the wind blows away.
Therefore the wicked
will not stand in the judgment,
nor sinners
in the assembly of the righteous.
For the Lord watches over
the way of the righteous,
but the way of the wicked
will perish.

The godly man may stray from the path, but he returns by the way to be reestablished. But the wicked man has no path to discover—his way has perished with him.

In reading the Psalms, notice this refrain. God always addresses either the righteous or the wicked. There is no middle ground.

Psalm 34

We will deal specifically with those passages that are the heart of the lessons in this psalm because of its length. Note verse 7:

The angel of the Lord
encamps around
Those who fear him,
and he delivers them.

This is not meant to be a sentimental saying to make us feel better. It is a lesson to be accepted and believed. The godly man has a right to expect deliverance because of verses 11-14:

Come, my children, listen to me;
I will teach you the fear of the Lord.
Whoever of you loves life
and desires to see many good days,
keep your tongue from evil
and your lips from speaking lies.
Turn from evil and do good;
seek peace and pursue it.

This sermon is so short and to the point; it needs no explanation.

The third lesson is recorded in verse 18:

The Lord is close to the brokenhearted
and saves those who are crushed in spirit.

Jesus repeated this message in Matthew 5:4:

Blessed are those who mourn,
for they will be comforted.

PSALM 37

Psalm 37 deals with instruction about godly wisdom. Again, we go to the heart of these 40 verses and underscore verses 3, 4, 8, 23, 24 respectively:

Trust in the Lord and do good;
dwell in the land
and enjoy safe pasture.
Delight yourself in the Lord
and he will give you
the desires of your heart.

Refrain from anger
and turn from wrath;
do not fret—
it leads only to evil.

If the Lord delights in a man's way,
he makes his steps firm;
though he stumble, he will not fall,
for the Lord upholds him with his hand.

A promise, a warning, and another promise—happy is the man who knows and practices all three.

PSALM 73

This psalm warns us of the danger of envying the wicked man when he seems to prosper. Verses 13-17 are the heart of the lesson:

Surely in vain
have I kept my heart pure;
in vain have I washed
my hands in innocence.
All day long I have been plagued;
I have been punished every morning. . . .
When I tried to understand all this,
it was oppressive to me
till I entered the sanctuary of God;
then I understood their final destiny.

Psalm 112

Psalm 112 is also an acrostic psalm, as we have already discussed. Now we will discuss the instructional element of verses 1, 2, 7, 8, 10.

Praise the Lord.
Blessed is the man
who fears the Lord,
who finds great delight
in his commands.
His children will be
mighty in the land;
the generation of the upright
will be blessed (vv. 1, 2).

When I last attended the International Assembly of the Church of God, I looked at the program, which contained the appointments and elections for the next two years. Suddenly I noticed a pattern. Covering the first names, I noticed that the generation of men with whom I had worked still had their names on the program. Only the first names were changed.

Those who had followed the Lord had children who had done the same.

The same thing is true on every level of the church where I have worked for almost 50 years. I hear a last name and I ask, "What relation are you to __________?" Then I find the lesson of Psalm 112—those who follow the Lord raise up a generation who also follow Him.

He will have no fear of bad news;
his heart is steadfast,
trusting in the Lord.
His heart is secure,
he will have no fear (vv. 7, 8).

The wicked man will see and be vexed,
he will gnash his teeth and waste away;
The longings of the wicked
will come to nothing (v. 10).

It has long been established that the high cost of government stems primarily in trying to control the offspring of the wicked.

Psalm 119

Since this psalm is also an acrostic, we have looked at it in detail in the previous section. We need to say here that it is a psalm of 176 verses—the longest book in the Bible—and in each verse the writer extols the Word of God. His intention was to place a synonym for the Word of God in each verse. Because it is one of the great teaching psalms, we should take time to absorb what it has to say about the Word of God.

In the first of 22 sections, the author uses the following

synonyms for "the Word": *law* (Torah), *statutes, ways, precepts, decrees, commands* . . . and repeats *laws* and *decrees* to complete the eight verses.

An interesting study would be to read the psalm in its entirety and discover the hidden elements. In verses 90, 121, 122 and 132, I could not identify the intention of the author. That does not mean that it is not there. It simply means that the Hebrew, having been translated into the Greek and then into the English, obscures the meaning. The fact that scholars do not have the original scroll makes the synonym sometimes more difficult to determine.

Psalm 133

This psalm teaches us about the beauty of unity among God's people. The opening verse states this theme:

> *How good and pleasant it is*
> *when brothers live*
> *together in unity!* (v. 1).

Anyone who believes that this is universal should spend one day in the office of a pastor.

> *It is like precious oil*
> *poured on the head,*
> *running down on the beard. . . .*
> *It is as if the dew of [Mount] Hermon*
> *were falling on Mount Zion.*
> *For there the Lord*
> *bestows his blessings,*
> *even life forevermore* (vv. 2, 3).

It is fitting to close the didactic section with this beautiful plea for unity. God's people today are divided, not only by name but also by doctrine. Because of this disunity, the unsaved have difficulty in believing because they do not know what to believe. But the promise of "even life forevermore" is a worthy reward for those who walk in harmony with all who love the Lord.

In closing this section, I hasten to add that some teaching can be found in most of the Psalms. Those we have called attention to seem to have been written especially as a teaching tool.

LITURGICAL SONGS AND PRAYERS

Liturgical songs and prayers are those compositions prepared for special occasions. Those generally listed as liturgical are Psalms 15, 24, 30, 45, 46, 68, 113-118. We will look at these in order.

PSALM 15

Psalm 15 is the picture of a perfect Israelite. We will not argue whether he ever existed; this is simply the picture of what he would be like if he did. The writer begins by asking, in essence: "Who is worthy to dwell where God is? Who is worthy to be called a true and genuine citizen of the kingdom of God?" (v. 1). The answers we find will set a standard the New Testament Christian would do well to imitate. We might today ask the question: Who will be ready to go with the Lord when He comes for His saints? That person will dwell with Him forever.

In the following verse, God begins to answer the question: "He whose walk is blameless and who does what is righteous, who speaks the truth from his heart" (v. 2). It is said that Thomas Jefferson called this psalm the picture of a true gentleman.

If we remember that this is a psalm of David, we may correctly suppose that indeed the psalmist does not know anyone like this. Some have thought the exact opposite is true. Some suggest that it may have been written when Absalom drove David from the throne. This would help us understand why David is asking where such a person might be found.

If so, we can understand his thinking that the person now dwelling there did not belong. Also, because of the complicity of those with Absalom, David could be saying that he wishes that there were those about him with these characteristics.

Verse 3 further develops the theme that the perfect man is the one "who does his neighbor no wrong," as had been David's lot. Verse 4 seems to emphasize the words, "Who keeps his oath even when it hurts." This could be understood as an indictment against those who had turned against David to support Absalom. Verse 5 adds that such a man could not be bribed with honor and position, such as Absalom had offered those who followed him.

The fact that the term *tabernacle* (KJV) is used seems to strengthen the Davidic authorship, although some want to place it at a much later date. The *New International Version* translates the word as "sanctuary" to make it universally applicable. To Christians, however, it is understood that the qualification has to do with heaven and those who would live with God forever. Although we do not know when it was written, it was obviously a song of the sanctuary, frequently sung.

Psalm 24

This psalm has a close affinity with the one just discussed. The title identifies it as a psalm of David. Clarke[1] places it about the 14th year of David's reign, when the Israelites were moving the ark of the Lord from the house of Obed-Edom. The circumstances are described in 2 Samuel 6. Remember, the Philistines had captured the ark while Eli was judge.

Many of the questions are almost the same as those in Psalm 15. In fact, we get the feeling that we may be reading an expanded version of Psalm 15. The opening establishes the reason for this all-important question.

> *The earth is the Lord's,*
> *and everything in it,*
> *the world, and all who live in it;*
> *for he founded it upon the seas*
> *and established it upon the waters* (vv. 1, 2).

Then in verse 3 we find the recurring question: "Who is worthy to dwell in God's Holy Place?" (paraphrased); literally, "stand in his holy place."

Delitzsch[2] believes the singing proceeded as follows. The festive procession stood below the hill of Zion. There they sang in chorus verses 1 and 2, quoted above.

A single voice then asks the question of who is able to stand in the hill of the Lord (v. 3). Another voice answers: "He who has clean hands and a pure heart . . ." (v. 4) and is joined by the chorus of verses 5 and 6.

The festive procession joins in to enter the citadel (v. 7):

> *Lift up your heads, O you gates;*
> *be lifted up, you ancient doors,*
> *that the King of glory may come in.*

Then, in verse 8, a voice from the gates calls: "Who is this King of glory?" After this, the chorus repeats the request given in verse 7 that the King of glory may be allowed to come in. The voice from the gates again asks: "Who is this King of glory?" The chorus responds then emphatically in verse 10:

The Lord Almighty—
he is the King of glory. Selah.

There is no doubt that this is an Old Testament prophecy of the coming advent of our Lord. Note Malachi 3:1: "'Then suddenly the Lord you are seeking will come to his temple; the messenger of the covenant, whom you desire, will come,' says the Lord Almighty."

Psalm 30

This song bears the title in the Hebrew as "A Song of the Dedication of the House." Some believe that the term *house* refers to the palace of David. If so, we would find the historical occasion in 2 Samuel 5:11: "Now Hiram king of Tyre sent messages to David, along with cedar logs and carpenters and stonemasons, and they built a palace for David." However, we cannot be certain that this is the house referred to in the title. In 2 Samuel 7, the house is referred to as the Temple which Solomon would build. In a real sense, this would be the house of David and the house of the Lord:

The Lord himself will establish a house for you:
When your days are over
and you rest with your fathers,
I will raise up your offspring
to succeed you,
who will come from your own body,

and I will establish his kingdom.
He is the one who will build a house
for my Name . . . (2 Samuel 7:11-13).

We cannot be certain of which house he is referring. Even those who write on the subject are equally divided. Let us see if the internal evidence sheds any light at all on the subject. If it was for the palace of David, it would be his prayer of dedication. If it was the Temple which Solomon would build, it would be David's rejoicing over what the Lord would do.

I will exalt you, O Lord,
for you lifted me out of the depths
and did not let my enemies gloat over me.
O Lord my God,
I called for you to help and you healed me.
O Lord, you brought me up from the grave;
you spared me from going
down into the pit (Psalm 30:1-3).

This does not sound like the opening lines of the Temple dedication, but it does sound like David, who had been spared from death by Saul and is now being established in a permanent dwelling. He then invites those about him to sing to the Lord:

Sing to the Lord, you saints of his;
praise his holy name.
For his anger lasts only a moment,
but his favor lasts a lifetime;
weeping may remain for a night,
but rejoicing comes in the morning (vv. 4, 5).

David was now certain that his time of fleeing the enemy was past and the bright day had dawned. He uses a parallelism by comparing a day with a lifetime and contrasting living under God's wrath with living in his mercies.

It is likely that the next verses record the error of David when he ordered a census and was given the wrath of God for a reward. In 1 Chronicles 21, we are told that the devil prompted this action. Even Joab, the leader of his army, warned against it. The purpose of the census was to count his fighting men, now that he had been victorious.

When I felt secure,
I said, "I shall never be shaken."
O Lord, when you favored me,
you made my mountain stand firm;
but when you hid your face,
I was dismayed.
To you, O Lord, I called;
to the Lord I cried for mercy:
"What gain is there in my destruction,
in my going down into the pit?
Will the dust praise you?
Will it proclaim your faithfulness?" (vv. 6-9).

The historical account does not tell us what was in David's heart when he decided to take the census, but verse 6 leaves no doubt. His pride in being the head of a great nation with a mighty fighting force made him the man of the universe in his mind.

He began with praise and ended with praise but, in Davidic manner, he expressed his grief at displeasing God. Having a strong army elevated his carnal nature to feel that he would always be secure. But when God sent His wrath, David again realized that there was no hope outside of God.

"Hear, O Lord, and be merciful to me;
O Lord, be my help."
You turned my wailing into dancing;
you removed my sackcloth
and clothed me with joy,
that my heart may sing to you
and not be silent.
O Lord my God,
I will give you thanks forever (vv. 10-12).

In 1 Chronicles 21:16, we are told that David and his elders actually wore sackcloth when they saw the angel of the Lord hovering over the city. No wonder his heart sang with joy. This does not sound like a traditional dedication prayer, such as we would expect today. But we must remember David was a man who was more interested in giving God the glory than receiving it himself. He had made that mistake once. Now on this dedication day, he wanted everyone to know both his pride (vv. 6, 7) and the sorrow it brought. On this special occasion he expressed his joy in the Lord. He did this at both the beginning and the ending of the prayer.

Psalm 45

When you read this psalm, it is easily seen as the wedding song of a king. The title includes the words "A Wedding Song." But the question of whose wedding is not so easily distinguished. Without a doubt, it was written to honor an earthly king as verse 2 indicates:

You are the most excellent of men
and your lips have been anointed with grace,
since God has blessed you forever.

Delitzsch[3] makes a case for Jehoram to be the king and that the poem presents him as a type of Christ. Matthew 1:8 places his name in the genealogy of Christ. He argues that the statement in Psalm 45:12, "The Daughter of Tyre will come with a gift," refers to Athaliah, whom Jehoram married. The fact that they failed to be faithful in their latter years would not disqualify them from being a type of Christ any more than Solomon, who remained a type in spite of his falling away.

Some have indeed held for a wedding of Solomon, but verse 16 seems to rule that out with the words "Your sons will take the place of your fathers." Solomon had a father, David, to whom he could look, but someone further down the line of Christ must have indeed been intended to require the plural form. In verse 10 the bride is admonished to "forget your people and your father's house." As a daughter of Tyre, she was to give up the old life and rejoice in the newfound groom, even as the Christian is to forsake the world for heavenly bliss.

In the final analysis, there is no doubt that the king represents the Christ who is to come and claim the throne of His father David and rule forever as the Son of God:

Your throne, O God,
will last for ever and ever;
a scepter of justice
will be the scepter of your kingdom (v. 6).

Note this connection in Hebrews 1:8:

But about the Son he says,
"Your throne, O God,
will last for ever and ever,
and righteousness
will be the scepter of your kingdom."

Also, we see this picture in Revelation 21:9, 10: "'Come, I will show you the bride, the wife of the Lamb' . . . and [the angel] showed me the Holy City, Jerusalem, coming down out of heaven from God." Remember that the New Jerusalem will be made up of Jews and Gentiles from all parts of the world. We should not be surprised that a descendant of David and daughter of a heathen king would serve as a type of that which will be.

Those who see a type of Christ interpret this psalm as follows: The psalm contains a beautiful description of the valor, justice and truth of the Divine Bridegroom and beauty of the Bride in verses 2-9. The address to the Bride by her companion is found in verses 10-15. The prediction of her numerous descendants are described in verses 16 and 17.

Psalm 46

This psalm is noted "For the director of music. Of the Sons of Korah. According to *alamoth*." We have already talked about the Sons of Korah. The exact meaning of the term *alamoth* in this setting cannot be determined, but it is obviously used as a musical term. The word in the Hebrew means "maidens" and could therefore carry the meaning of "a song for sopranos." It has been called "Zion's Battle Song" and describes a people who feel secure in their trust in God while people all around are in turmoil. It is said to have been the basis of the hymn written by Martin Luther, "A Mighty Fortress Is Our God," which was the song of the Reformation.

> *God is our refuge and strength,*
> *an ever-present help in trouble.*
> *Therefore we will not fear,*
> *though the earth give way and the*
> *mountains fall into the heart of the sea,*
> *though its waters roar*
> *and foam and the mountains quake*
> *with their surging. Selah* (Psalm 46:1-3).

It is easy enough to picture the upheaval of nature in these verses. The writer may have had this in mind, but it is just as likely that he was referring to the social and spiritual upheaval going on around him.

> *There is a river whose streams*
> *make glad the city of God,*
> *the holy place where the Most High dwells.*
> *God is within her,*
> *she will not fall;*
> *God will help her at break of day.*
> *Nations are in uproar,*
> *kingdoms fall;*
> *he lifts his voice,*
> *the earth melts.*
> *The Lord Almighty is with us;*
> *the God of Jacob is our fortress.*
> *Selah* (vv. 4-7).

The phrase "nations are in uproar" suggests that there is more to the meaning than a natural catastrophe. The same description could be written in 1999 and be just as appropriate. What we wish we could say is that "God is with us." There is no center of quiet confidence in this portion of the song. The river that makes glad the city of God still flows in the heart of His people, but there is no nation or city that is so blessed—not even the earthly Zion.

Come and see the works of the Lord,
the desolations he has brought
on the earth (v. 8).

War has literally destroyed the earth. Only Zion stands as a stronghold. Was the writer referring to conditions as they were, or as they would be some day? Both are acceptable interpretations, since we have not been able to establish a date for the writing. Perhaps both better convey the writer's intent.

He makes wars cease to the ends of the earth;
he breaks the bow and shatters the spear,
he burns the shields with fire (v. 9).

Here he speaks of the future when Zion shall be at peace. At that time God will put an end to war throughout the land. The phrase "burns the shields with fire" speaks of another day.

"Be still, and know that I am God;
I will be exalted among the nations,
I will be exalted in the earth."
The Lord Almighty is with us;
the God of Jacob is our fortress.
Selah (vv. 10, 11).

Thus it once was and thus, in a more perfect sense, will it be at His coming.

PSALM 68

This psalm is titled as a psalm and song of David. This title places a little more emphasis on the song element than is present in some psalms. Not all psalms are to be sung; some are prayers that may have on some occasion been sung, but you could hardly expect to go into the Temple and hear David's prayer of confession of his sin with Bathsheba (Psalm 51). This composition, however, is meant to be sung.

The theme is centered around the care and deliverance of God's people, Israel. What may be foreshadowed here is the final triumph of Christ over His enemies and the final destruction of evil. Henry H. Halley[4] tells us that this battle march was a favorite of the Crusaders, the Huguenots, Savonarola, and Oliver Cromwell. There are many theories concerning the circumstances of this psalm, and for this reason Ellicott[5] suggests that we stay with what can be textually supported.

1. The mention of the Temple in verse 29 certainly places the psalm subsequent to Solomon. Although the Temple was built in his lifetime, his rule (or reign) was full of peace and not war.

2. The poet makes free use of older songs. In fact, some have called it a poem of "lyric fragments." When we read Judges 5, we find much of the inspiration that has gone into this composition. This is the magnificent song of Deborah when God gave Israel victory over Jabin, the king of Canaan. This connection does not detract from the psalm, because many psalms contain fragments of other psalms, as well as songs about historical accounts.

3. Ellicott[6] points out that verses 4-7 and 21 are veritable historic portraits of God's victories over Edom, the exploits of Shamgar and Jael, and the victory over the Canaanite kings when the stars fought against Sisera.

4. In this song the Temple is represented as a place of reverence where foreign powers bring gifts.

5. The warlike tempo of this poem seems not to have arisen out of a particular battle, but rather verses 5, 10, 19 and 20 suggest that it carries a strong confidence in God to deliver in any and all circumstances.

As tempting as it may be to get carried into every street and avenue of this poetic pathway, the reader may want to concentrate on the blessedness of God's power to deliver in every circumstance. Verses 34 and 35 emphasize the theme we have followed throughout the Psalms:

Proclaim the power of God,
whose majesty is over Israel,
whose power is in the skies.
You are awesome, O God,
in your sanctuary;
the God of Israel
gives power and strength
to his people.

PASSOVER PSALMS (PSALMS 113—118)

Psalm 113

Although we will address some of the Passover Psalms separately, there is a good reason for looking at them together as we begin our study. These psalms taken together are what is known as the great Hallel sung at the most solemn festivals, especially the Passover Feast. The word *Hallel* in the Hebrew means "praise." It is part of that combination with which we are so familiar—*hallelujah* (often spelled *halleluyah*), which means "praise God."

The Full Life Study Bible tells us in its notes that the six psalms together are regarded as one great hymn. Matthew 26:30 tells us that after Jesus had completed His Passover meal, they sang a hymn and then they went out. It was customary that before the meal, they would sing Psalms 113 and 114, and at the close of the meal the families would sing Psalms 115, 116, 117 and 118. These psalms became so much a part of the Passover observance that in the time of Matthew they were known as a hymn.

All these psalms are untitled except for the word *hallelujah* in the original Hebrew. Since Psalm 113 was the first psalm of the Passover, it is appropriate that it begins with a praise to God.

> *Praise the Lord.*
> *Praise, O servants of the Lord,*
> *praise the name of the Lord.*
> *Let the name of the Lord be praised,*
> *both now and forevermore.*
> *From the rising of the sun*
> *to the place where it sets,*
> *the name of the Lord is to be praised.*
> *The Lord is exalted over all the nations,*
> *his glory above the heavens.*
> *Who is like the Lord our God,*
> *the One who sits enthroned on high,*

who stoops down to look
on the heavens and the earth? (vv. 1-6).

The psalm continues, very appropriately for the Passover, with a prayer for the poor and needy:

He raises the poor from the dust
and lifts the needy from the ash heap;
he seats them with princes,
with the princes of their people.
He settles the barren woman in her home
as a happy mother of children.
Praise the Lord (vv. 7-9).

PSALM 114

Psalm 114 deals directly with what we would expect to find in the Passover song:

When Israel came out of Egypt,
the house of Jacob
from a people of a foreign tongue,
Judah became God's sanctuary,
Israel his dominion (vv. 1, 2).

The remaining portion of the psalm tells of God's wondrous deliverance from the land of Egypt and is to be understood as a figure of speech often used in poetry.

The sea looked and fled,
the Jordan turned back;
the mountains skipped like rams,
the hills like lambs.
Why was it, O sea, that you fled,

O Jordan, that you turned back,
you mountains, that you skipped like rams,
you hills, like lambs?
Tremble, O earth,
at the presence of the Lord,
at the presence of the God of Jacob,
who turned the rock into a pool,
the hard rock into springs of water (vv. 5-8).

The Passover was the first of three annual feasts celebrated. It was also known as the Feast of Unleavened Bread (Exodus 23:15). The festival began on the 14th day of Abib in the Hebrew calendar. It became the first month in the year, to commemorate the coming out of Egypt. Since the Hebrew months followed the moon and our calendar does not, the exact date in modern times is not easy to determine, but it may fall in either March or April. According to Esther 3:7, *Abib* became known as *Nisan* after the Captivity.

The paschal supper consisted of lamb and bitter herbs with unleavened bread and wine. The word *wine* here meant specifically the juice of the grape. Jesus called attention to this distinction in Matthew 26:29 when He said, "I tell you, I will not drink of this fruit of the vine from now on until that day when I drink it anew . . . in my Father's kingdom."

Psalm 115

The after-supper songs consisted of Psalm 115-118, the hymn to which Matthew referred. Psalm 115 begins by declaring the glory of God:

Not to us, O Lord, not to us

but to your name be the glory,
because of your love and faithfulness.
Why do the nations say,
"Where is their God?"
Our God is in heaven;
he does whatever pleases him (vv. 1-3).

This is followed by the declaration of the vanity of idols:

But their idols are silver and gold,
made by the hands of men.
They have mouths, but cannot speak,
eyes, but they cannot see;
they have ears, but cannot hear,
noses, but they cannot smell;
they have hands, but cannot feel,
feet, but they cannot walk;
nor can they utter a sound with their throats.
Those who make them will be like them,
and so will all who trust in them (vv. 4-8).

Israel had learned the idol lesson the hard way. From Sinai, when Aaron made the golden calf, Israel lapsed into idolatry until the whole northern kingdom was overrun by the Assyrians. The prophets then thought Judah would have learned a lesson. But it was not until Babylon destroyed the Temple and took the southern kingdom into captivity that Israel learned that God would not tolerate idols. Our Protestant churches may hang pictures on the wall, but never in a synagogue does anyone find the likeness of "anything in heaven above or on the earth beneath or in the waters below," as commanded in Exodus 20:4. Israel's lesson against idolatry was learned forever.

O house of Israel,
trust in the Lord—
he is their help and shield.
O house of Aaron,
trust in the Lord—
he is their help and shield.
You who fear him,
trust in the Lord—
he is their help and shield (Psalm 115:9-11).

The exhortation to trust in the Lord is found in these verses. It is interesting to note that the material found here also appears in Psalm 135:15-20. The fact that they both deal with abstaining from idols is not a coincidence. The writer then extols the goodness of God unto His people:

The Lord remembers us and will bless us:
He will bless the house of Israel,
he will bless the house of Aaron,
he will bless those who fear the Lord—
small and great alike.
May the Lord make you increase,
both you and your children.
May you be blessed by the Lord,
the Maker of heaven and earth (115:12-15).

The psalm ends with the thought that since the dead could not praise the Lord, the living should:

The highest heavens belong to the Lord,
but the earth he has given to man.
It is not the dead who praise the Lord,
those who go down to silence;

it is we who extol the Lord,
both now and forevermore.
Praise the Lord (vv. 16-18).

Psalm 116

In Psalm 116, the psalmist praises God because he has escaped from death:

I love the Lord, for he heard my voice;
he heard my cry for mercy.
Because he turned his ear to me,
I will call on him as long as I live (vv. 1, 2).

The writer extols the goodness of God in saving those who called on Him:

Then I called on the name of the Lord:
"O Lord, save me!"
The Lord is gracious and righteous;
our God is full of compassion.
The Lord protects the simplehearted;
when I was in great need, he saved me (vv. 4-6).

The writer emphasizes that God has delivered him from death as well as from sorrow and failure.

For you, O Lord,
have delivered my soul from death,
my eyes from tears,
my feet from stumbling,
that I may walk before the Lord
in the land of the living (vv. 8, 9).

The psalmist then meditates on how he can repay the Lord. This he cannot do, but he can be loyal in his vows and give voice to the salvation God has brought to him:

How can I repay the Lord
for all his goodness to me?
I will lift up the cup of salvation
and call on the name of the Lord.
I will fulfill my vows to the Lord
in the presence of his people.
Precious in the sight of the Lord
is the death of his saints.
O Lord, truly I am your servant;
I am your servant,
the son of your maidservant;
you have freed me from my chains (vv. 12-16).

The author asks in verse 12 how he can ever repay God's mercy. In this psalm, we also find the thought so comforting when facing death or experiencing the death of a loved one: "Precious in the sight of the Lord is the death of his saints" (v. 15).

In the closing verses, the psalmist emphasizes that his sacrifice will be a thank offering to God, and the chapter ends with a hallelujah or praise to God:

I will sacrifice a thank offering to you
and call on the name of the Lord.
I will fulfill my vows to the Lord
in the presence of all his people,
in the courts of the house of the Lord—
in your midst, O Jerusalem.
Praise the Lord (vv. 17-19).

Psalm 117

Psalm 117 is the shortest chapter in the Bible. It praises God because His mercy extends to all nations. How strange that must be for an Israelite to sing, because Israel saw God as their God. But how very appropriate that Christ sang it with His disciples the night He went to the cross to pay for the sins of all mankind.

Praise the Lord, all you nations;
extol him, all you peoples.
For great is his love toward us,
and the faithfulness of the Lord
endures forever.
Praise the Lord (vv. 1, 2).

Psalm 118

We believe that Psalm 118 was the last song Jesus sang with His disciples on this earth. We would do well to read and meditate on it. Verses 1-4 begin with an exhortation to praise God for His mercy:

Give thanks to the Lord,
for he is good;
his love endures forever.
Let Israel say:
"His love endures forever."
Let the house of Aaron say:
"His love endures forever."
Let those who fear the Lord say:
"His love endures forever."

Following are the advantages of serving God, as the psalmist declares his trust in God:

In my anguish I cried to the Lord,
and he answered by setting me free.
The Lord is with me;
I will not be afraid.
What can man do to me? (vv. 5, 6).

He further describes the way his enemies encompassed him. But he praises God for His mercy:

I was pushed back and about to fall,
but the Lord helped me.
The Lord is my strength and my song;
he has become my salvation (vv. 13, 14).

How wonderful that on this fateful night, Jesus sang verses 19 and 20:

Open for me the gates of righteousness;
I will enter and give thanks to the Lord.
This is the gate of the Lord
through which the righteous may enter.

It is also here that we find the prophetic words in verses 22 and 23:

The stone the builders rejected
has become the capstone;
the Lord has done this,
and it is marvelous in our eyes.

See also Matthew 21:42. Can anyone doubt that Christ understood the significance of what He sang that night?

The psalmist closes this song by singing about the day of the Lord and blessing the One who comes in the name of the Lord:

This is the day the Lord has made;
let us rejoice and be glad in it.
O Lord, save us;
O Lord, grant us success.
Blessed is he who comes
in the name of the Lord.
From the house of the Lord
we bless you (vv. 24-26).

How many in Jerusalem realized that this was the day of the Lord and they should have rejoiced in it? We can be certain that Christ understood His closing song with His disciples.

4

THE IMPRECATORY ELEMENTS IN PSALMS

Perhaps the first thing we need to do is talk about the problem of finding in the Psalms—a book of praises and prayers—what is called "imprecatory elements." The term suggests prayers for evil rather than for good. Some find it difficult to accept a man of God, such as David, praying for evil to come upon his enemies. The New Testament teaches us to love our enemies and to do good to them that persecute us. Are such passages consistent with the inspiration of the Spirit? Can we say that the entire Book of Psalms is inspired, when it contains prayers for God's wrath upon men? We will say more about this after looking at the passages that carry these elements.

We must first understand that we refer to these as "imprecatory elements" rather than "imprecatory psalms," because they are, for the most part, short prayers for God's destruction of the enemy. We will look at these and comment on the imprecatory elements as they occur.

PSALM 3

This psalm is a good example of the past tense, rather than the present or future tense of certain verbs. This is often a problem that translators face from the very opening words of Genesis. We must point out that Hebrew is one of the world's oldest languages, and some words may be used without a distinction of tenses. We note that this problem may cause translators to use a somewhat different interpretation.

This is one of the reasons why our translations differ, and we must choose what we believe to be the original meaning. One good example of this is the discussion that follows Psalm 3:7. Both the *New American Standard Bible* and the King James Version read in the past tense:

Arise, O Lord;
save me, O my God!
For Thou hast smitten
all my enemies
on the cheek;
Thou hast shattered
the teeth of the wicked (v. 7).

This places the acts of God's deliverance in the past and seem not to be offensive to us, because if God did it, that ends the matter. However, the *New International Version* introduces a distinctly imprecatory element in its petition for the Lord to do what the other two versions say God has already done:

Arise, O Lord!
Deliver me, O my God!

Strike all my enemies
on the jaw;
break the teeth of the wicked (v. 7).

We see, then, the same Hebrew text can be translated with a different emphasis, even though both translations are technically correct. With this in mind, let us then look at Psalm 3:7 with the thought that it could be imprecatory in nature.

This is the prayer of a righteous man driven from his throne by those who sought to claim not only the throne but also his life. Note here that he does not ask for their destruction, perhaps because his son Absalom was in the group. His first prayer in verse 7 is for his own deliverance. Then he prays for his enemies to be stricken, not in death, but a blow to their face so that their teeth would fall out. This was not a prayer of destruction, but more like the boxer in the ring who would give his opponent a solid blow. David is asking God to come and fight for him and win the victory. It is not an unseemly prayer, given the circumstance. This was not the prayer of an angry man. Immediately he turns to God with a request—for His blessings on His people.

Psalm 7

This is a prayer David sang unto the Lord concerning a Benjamite. This setting is found in 1 Samuel 24—26, where David twice spared the life of Saul and refused to kill him because he held an office that required God's anointing. David knew Saul would not stop trying to kill him, even though David refused to take Saul's life.

Arise, O Lord,
in Thine anger;

Lift up Thyself against
the rage of my adversaries,
And arouse Thyself for me;
Thou hast appointed judgment (v. 6).

Here David asks for justice. Certainly he should not be condemned for that request.

He has dug a pit
and hollowed it out,
And has fallen into
the hole which he made.
His mischief will return
upon his own head,
And his violence will descend
upon his own pate (vv. 15, 16).

Some translators regard this as a prayer for destruction. The *New International Version* makes it plain that David is stating a principle by which God deals with the wicked, and asks that it be put into practice.

PSALM 10

This psalm is a cry for help from the heart and lips of David. He is distressed because God has waited so long to come to his rescue.

Break the arm of
the wicked and the evildoer,
Seek out his wickedness until
Thou dost find none (v. 15).

What may seem like a prayer out of place for a righteous man is really a request for God to do what He planned to do for the wicked. These are not just unrighteous men, but those who are cruel even to the innocent and the peace loving. Note the accusations the psalmist brought against them before he makes this request of God:

For the wicked boasts
of his heart's desire (v. 3).

His mouth is full of curses
and deceit
and oppression (v. 7).

He lurks in a hiding place
as a lion in his lair . . .
He catches the afflicted
when he draws him
into his net.
He crouches, he bows down,
And the unfortunate fall
by his mighty ones (vv. 9, 10).

Should such a man not be called into account for his wickedness? Should not a man have his strength broken, as the request for his arm (v. 15) seems to indicate? This is an imprecatory element, but certainly does not seem like an unrighteous request.

Psalm 35

Let those be ashamed and dishonored
who seek my life;
Let those be turned back and humiliated
who devise evil against me.
Let them be like chaff before the wind,

With the angel of the Lord
driving them on.
Let their way be dark and slippery,
With the angel of the Lord
pursuing them (vv. 4-6).

Let destruction
come upon him unawares;
And let the net which he hid
catch himself;
Into that very destruction
let him fall (v. 8).

We soon see that the foe of the psalmist is also the foe of God. David had been chosen to protect the people of God, and although we do not know the specific occasion, he has a right to ask God to defeat his foes. Doesn't a king have a right to protect his people? Does he not also have a right to ask for God's help in doing so?

Psalm 55

This psalm is titled "A Maskil of David." The term *maskil* is found in the title of 13 psalms. It's exact meaning is subject to interpretation. In some cases it seems to have reference to a musical term while in others it is deemed to explain the type of psalm. The Greek translation identifies it as "a psalm of understanding." The participle form of this word is used in 2 Chronicles 30:22 to mean "those who play skillfully with good taste." It could then be rendered "a skillful song" of David. Some refute the authorship of David, but none are conclusive. What we do know from internal evidence is that the author was under oppression as revealed in verses 4 and 5:

My heart is in anguish within me,
And the terrors of death
have fallen upon me.
Fear and trembling come upon me.
And horror has overwhelmed me.

This is not a fear of the battle, because David had fought Goliath with the assurance that with God you can survive. His heart was never weak in battle, because he testified that God had trained his hands for war and his fingers for battle (Psalm 144:1). But who has not known the trembling of the heart when the enemy is unseen and untouchable?

His real desire was to flee away and be in the wilderness alone (55:7). This option was not available to him. He was compassed about with iniquity and mischief (v. 10). Oppression and deceit never leave the streets (v. 11). We do not know of a time in David's history when his administration was in such disarray.

Little is written about the reaction of the people after the Bathsheba affair. It is very possible that those of his administration turned, as have others at other times, to stir up strife. We are told that these were his close companions who now sought to destroy him.

For it is not an enemy
who reproaches me,
Then I could bear it;
Nor is it one who hates me
who has exalted himself against me,
Then I could hide myself from him.
But it is you, a man my equal,
My companion and

my familiar friend.
We who had
sweet fellowship together,
Walked in the house of God
in the throng (vv. 12-14).

Most of us have felt the sting of betrayal by a friend who was so close that he seemed like a brother. Now he or she is making every effort to destroy you—your reputation, your position of leadership—and alienate you from all your other friends. There is absolutely nothing you can do about it. All the accusations are based on lies, but you cannot disprove them because they are done secretly. Would you not turn to God for deliverance? The psalmist did. At first he speaks in a strong and bitter language:

Let death come deceitfully upon them;
Let them go down alive to Sheol,
For evil is in their dwelling,
in their midst (v. 15).

Then the Lord speaks to a man in his bitterness as He did in this psalm, and brings not only peace to his heart but also a blessed word that has comforted many of our hearts in times of trouble:

Cast your burden upon the Lord,
and He will sustain you;
He will never allow the righteous
to be shaken (v. 22).

If there is a lesson to be learned, and there is, it is the lesson that the devil can tie no knot that God cannot unravel.

Psalm 58

This psalm is a prayer for the destruction of the wicked. There may seem to be some irony in the fact that the *New International Version* includes in the title that the psalm is to be sung to the tune of "Do Not Destroy." It was a common practice for a songwriter to use a familiar tune to write his song. In fact, Psalms 57—59 are all written to the same tune.

Some scholars believe the setting is based on David's experience when Absalom seized the throne. There seems to be little that forces such a position. The psalmist develops his entire theme on the concept that there is a difference between the righteous and the wicked and that God will destroy the wicked without mercy.

> *O God, shatter their teeth*
> *in their mouth;*
> *Break out the fangs*
> *of the young lions, O Lord.*
> *Let them flow away*
> *like water that runs off;*
> *When he aims his arrows,*
> *let them be as headless shafts* (vv. 6, 7).

The prayer here is for the Lord to hasten His plans for the wicked. The psalmist also reminds the Lord that He is a righteous judge.

> *The righteous will rejoice*
> *when he sees vengeance.*
> *"Surely there is a God*
> *who judges on the earth!"* (vv. 10, 11).

Psalm 59

Psalm 59 has its historical setting in 1 Samuel 19, when Saul had sent men to David's house to kill him. In its broad view, we may regard this as a psalm based on evil men planning to lie in wait for an innocent man.

Clarke[1] argues for the authorship of Jeremiah and places this psalm around 445 B.C., when Nehemiah was endeavoring to rebuild the walls of Jerusalem. Sanballat the Hornite, Tobiah the Ammonite, and Geshem the Arabian watched day and night for ways to interfere with the work. Indeed they tried to lie in wait for Nehemiah so they could kill him and cause the work to cease.

His argument is entirely based on internal evidence, and might be acceptable if it was not titled to David. Although these titles are not part of the original inspired text, they were present when the Greek translation was made about 250 B.C. There is strength to the argument that much of the psalm is consistent with Psalm 58, also attributed to David and not challenged by Clarke. We should accept the titles, unless there is irrefutable internal evidence to the contrary.

In dealing with the imprecatory elements, the setting is the same: Evil men are seeking to destroy the life of a man who is called to do God's work. The question is, "Does a good man have the right, or the necessity laid upon him, to pray that God will hinder, or even destroy, the evildoers?" If not, then there is a problem with the inspiration of these psalms. I hold to the right and necessity of such a prayer and will argue the point at the close of this section.

In the first seven verses, the psalmist describes his wicked enemies and prays for God's deliverance from them. In verse 2, he even describes them as "bloodthirsty men"

(*NIV*), suggesting that it was his very life that was at stake. In verses 3 and 4 he pleads his own innocence: "Not for my transgression nor for my sin, O Lord, for no guilt of mine, they run and set themselves against me." And in verse 5, he pleads that the Lord will show no mercy to the wicked.

In verses 8–10, he expresses strong faith in God that indeed should be the attitude of everyone who prays in such a manner. "O my Strength," he cries in verse 9, "I watch for you; you, O God, are my fortress, my loving God" (*NIV*). These are not the words of an angry man, as some have argued, but the strong cry of a man of faith who believes in God's deliverance.

Do not slay them,
lest my people forget;
Scatter them by Thy power,
and bring them down,
O Lord, our shield.
On account of
the sin of their mouth
and the words of their lips,
Let them even be
caught in their pride,
And on account of curses
and lies which they utter.
Destroy them in wrath,
destroy them,
that they may be no more;
That men may know
that God rules in Jacob,
To the ends of the earth.
Selah.

And they return at evening,
they howl like a dog,
And go around the city.
They wander about for food,
And growl if they
are not satisfied (vv. 11-15).

In verses 11–15, he describes what he is asking God to do to his enemies. These are not the words of a bloodthirsty man, but a cry for the debasement of those who have exalted themselves against God. In the closing verses (16, 17), he praises God for the many blessings he has already received and expresses his determination to continue to trust Him.

But as for me,
I shall sing of Thy strength;
Yes, I shall joyfully sing
of Thy lovingkindness
in the morning . . . (v. 16).

PSALM 69

Psalm 69 expresses intense suffering. Like Psalm 22, it is often clear that the suffering describes the Messiah. This does not mean that the writer intended to write about the Messiah, and was probably not aware when the Holy Spirit broke in. Because a chapter on the fulfillment of prophecies from the Book of Psalms will be included, we will not deal with those at this time. However, for your own reference as you read this psalm, it will help to know that at least four verses—4, 9, 21 and 22—have been identified as prophetic by some scholars.

As to the title, I agree with Clarke[2] that this could not be a psalm of David, even though the *New International Version* and the *New American Standard Bible* both describe it as such. The title is very old, prior to A.D. 250, but the evidence that it is Davidic must be weighed against the internal evidence, which places it during the time of the Babylonian Captivity.

For God will save Zion
and build the cities of Judah,
That they may dwell there
and possess it.
And the descendants of
His servants will inherit it,
And those who love His name
will dwell in it (vv. 35, 36).

It must be admitted that these two verses, at least, were written after the destruction of the city of Jerusalem, and after Judah had been laid waste by the Babylonians. This does not mean, however, that David could not have written the bulk of the psalm and these verses later attached by an unknown author. By the Spirit, David could have written the prophecy of the rebuilding of Judah, but that is something that should not be forced upon the text.

When I wept in my soul with fasting,
It became my reproach.
When I made sackcloth my clothing,
I became a byword to them.
Those who sit in the gate
talk about me,
And I am the song of the drunkards (vv. 10-12).

Pour out Thine indignation on them,
And may Thy burning anger
overtake them (v. 24).

These may well be prophetic declarations as to what would happen to Judah. Certainly much of the psalm is prophetic in nature.

Do Thou add iniquity
to their iniquity,
And may they not come
into Thy righteousness.
May they be blotted out
of the book of life,
And may they not be recorded
with the righteous (vv. 27, 28).

If these should stand as prayers, they would be difficult to handle. The truth is, there are some who will not share in God's salvation and whose name will not be listed with the righteous. Psalm 1 teaches us that there are only two types of people—the righteous and the wicked. That psalm describes the destiny of both. It will help us to understand that this passage is just as legitimate as Psalm 1. There is nothing new in the concept that the cruel, the oppressor, the scorner and the hypocrite shall have none of God's blessings in this life and shall be excluded from the kingdom of God for eternity.

Psalm 109

This psalm deals with the fate of God's adversaries. Judas seems to enter the picture in verse 8. It is necessary then to regard some of the wrath to come as prophecy, as well as prayers for their fulfillment. The psalmist does not hesitate to speak against his enemies and to pray for God's judgment upon them.

They have also surrounded me
with words of hatred,
And fought against me
without cause (v. 3).

Thus they repaid me evil for good,
And hatred for my love.
Appoint a wicked man over him (vv. 5, 6).

Let his days be few;
Let another take his office (v. 8).

Verse 8 seems to have a New Testament fulfillment in Judas but, like many prophecies, probably has a more immediate application. The latter part of the psalm explains why these requests are worded so strongly:

Because he did not remember
to show lovingkindness,
But persecuted the afflicted
and needy man,
And the despondent in heart,
to put them to death.
He also loved cursing,
so it came to him (vv. 16, 17).

Such prayers and prophecies in the psalms are not without cause. The writer takes great care to establish that it is not just a matter of personal dislike. This psalm will be explored more in the section on New Testament fulfillment of prophecies from the Book of Psalms.

Psalm 129

This psalm is included in the songs of ascents, but one section should be noted as imprecatory:

May all who hate Zion,
Be put to shame
and turned backward,
Let them be like grass
upon the housetops,
Which withers before it grows up;
With which the reaper
does not fill his hand,
Or the binder of sheaves his bosom;
Nor do those who pass by say,
"The blessing of the Lord be upon you;
We bless you in the name of the Lord" (vv. 5-8).

This is the future for those who hate Zion. The "grass upon the housetops" refers to the sod covering many ancient buildings. The lives of the wicked will be as useless as the dried grass. The reaper will pass it by.

The last verse refers to the custom of the Old Testament in pronouncing God's blessings upon those who pass by. We still use the phrase "God bless you," especially to those we know in the Lord. Here, the psalmist says that this salutation shall not be made to those who hate Zion.

Psalm 137

This is a historical psalm, and the imprecatory elements have to do with prayer for God's judgment on those who killed and destroyed in a wanton and merciless way.

O daughter of Babylon,
you devastated one,
How blessed will be the one
who repays you
With the recompense
with which you have repaid us.
How blessed will be
the one who seizes and dashes
your little ones
Against the rock (vv. 8, 9).

It is easy to criticize such a prayer if one has not experienced such treatment. I see no evidence that God's ear was closed to such petitions. Babylon had done more than take a city—it had ruthlessly destroyed the inhabitants. In fact, history tells us that this is what happened to Babylon when it was overrun, as prophesied by Isaiah 13:16 and Jeremiah 23:2.

Psalm 139

For the most part, this psalm extolls the omniscience of God. In His infinite knowledge, every thought and word is known by Him (see vv. 1-12). In the following section (vv. 13-18) the writer continues to magnify God in relation to man's origin. It is in the third section (vv. 19-24), that we face the reality of his imprecatory writing and come face-to-face with the author's feeling about those who stand against God and His servants—including the writer of this psalm (vv. 19- 24). We will note only the most severe segments of this section.

O that Thou wouldst slay
the wicked, O God . . .

For they speak
against Thee wickedly,
And Thine enemies take
Thy name in vain.
Do I not hate
those who hate
Thee, O Lord? . . .
I hate them
with the utmost hatred;
They have become my enemies (vv. 19-22).

Who among us has not envisioned a world in which the wicked would be removed and only the righteous remain? Is this prayer any more foreign to the Christian today than it is to the Old Testament saint? Is it wrong to ask God to hasten such a world? This is exactly what we envision at the coming of Christ. The wicked will be slain in a battle where Christ leads the forces of righteousness to triumph over the wicked.

We would do the psalmist an injustice if we closed this section without noting his closing prayer, in which he opens his own heart to God:

Search me, O God,
and know my heart;
Try me and know
my anxious thoughts;
And see if there be
any hurtful way in me,
And lead me in
the everlasting way (vv. 23, 24).

Summary of Comments about Imprecatory Elements

The following are arguments set forth to assist the reader in understanding the underlying principles that relate to the imprecatory elements:

1. God has determined evil for the wicked and security for the righteous. It is not wrong to pray for such.
2. Some imprecatory elements are prophetic in nature. The Spirit prompts the prayer because God has already determined it.
3. Some elements ask for justice when the wicked have done wickedly—such as dashing babies against stone walls and crushing their heads during the destruction of Jerusalem.
4. The only section in which forgiveness is asked to be withheld seems to relate to Judas, and this was determined in the foreknowledge of God.
5. It is good for the Christian to understand personal forgiveness and national leadership responsibility.
    a. Was Joshua wrong to fight a war of aggression against the Canaanites, even though God had specifically commanded it? Did Israel have a right and responsibility to pray for victory and destruction of the enemy?
    b. Jesus never taught, so far as it can be determined, about the responsibility of the Christian in case of an invading enemy.
    c. Jesus' message in the New Testament was person-to-person. No advice was given to God-fearing world rulers. It seems the standard of nations and their rulers was set in the Old

Testament. Can a Christian president of the United States fail to take up arms to protect his people? Not likely.

d. Can Christian judges simply forgive a serial murderer? Does the New Testament require this any more than the Old?
e. Can a Christian be a police officer? If so, what does he do when called to a schoolyard where eight have been killed and many more wounded? Does he wait until the individual with the AK-47 runs out of bullets, or does he kill him on the spot to stop the murders?
f. Under any government, does the New Testament require drunk drivers and terrorists to be turned loose on citizens who look to government for protection?

6. Will God not one day divide the wicked from the righteous and send them to their eternal destruction? This is a New Testament picture.
7. Will not the greatest war of the world, which will kill millions, be led by Christ himself? This is no plea for hatred and unbridled destruction. Can we condemn the Christian for praying for what God has already determined?
8. What was the attitude of Christians during World War II? Were they forbidden to pray for the death and destruction of Adolph Hitler and those who supported him? Could they not pray for the success of the armies trying to stop a mad ruler?

The arguments above are given to demonstrate that some have taken a simple statement about loving our enemies and tied it to all the cruelty of the world. Christ did not do that, and we should be careful in remembering that duties never conflict. We love our neighbors even though they may be our enemies. However, if they enter our home to kill our family, our responsibility changes.

5

SONGS OF THE PILGRIMAGES

Psalms 120-134 are commonly known as Pilgrim Songs. In some translations and versions, this group is called Songs of Ascents.

Ellicott[1] uses the title "Songs of Degrees," which is a translation from the Septuagint, "of steps," which literally means "to go up." One view is that these 15 psalms are songs chanted by the caravans as they journeyed to Jerusalem to the three yearly feasts: the Passover, the Feast of Harvest, and the Feast of Tabernacles (also called the Feast of Ingathering). At these feasts, every adult male was expected to appear before the Lord (Exodus 23:17).

Some effort has been made to establish these psalms in the period following the return from the Exile and the ascent back to Jerusalem. There is limited evidence for this second view, although Tilling (Delitzsch[2]) makes a case for it.

A third view associates the 15 psalms with the 15 steps that led into the sanctuary. The fact that there were indeed 15 steps lends credence to this view. Ellicott[3] says that the

Talmud claims that these psalms were sung on each of the steps.

Of the three, the first description seems more reasonable to me. In ascending to Jerusalem, we went by bus, but the guide stopped in appointed places and we read (rather than sang) the psalms. Somehow it is easy to envision the long trek of several miles up a very steep hill. Those who walked in those days would certainly have appointed resting places. How natural it would be for a worshiper to sing at each stop before continuing the journey. In reality, whether or not the problem is resolved to everyone's satisfaction, the value of the 15 songs is not diminished.

One might be led to think that if they were written to be sung in the same setting, they would all have the same theme. But this is not the case. The author of these psalms is unknown. We do not even know if they were all written by the same author. They might well be a collection of songs from more than one writer. Clarke[4] points out that some have been ascribed to David, Solomon, Ezra, Haggai, Zechariah and to Malachi, without any positive evidence. There is no question that we have an excellent group of songs of great importance and that they were of much encouragement to those who sung them. We will identify each psalm and deal with what is known about it.

Psalm 120

The first of the Songs of Ascents is an earnest prayer for protection for those who lived far from Zion, among treacherous and deceitful people. The writer makes it a first-person experience, but it is a potent reminder of those who, at one time perhaps, lived in Babylon, far from Zion.

Woe is me,
for I sojourn in Meshech,
For I dwell among
the tents of Kedar!
Too long has my soul
had its dwelling
With those who
hate peace (vv. 5, 6).

Meshech is often associated with tribes living along the borders of Armenia, while Kedar is more often associated with Arabia (Ellicott[5]). Since they are separated at such a distance, the poet may be using them as a type of savage existence. This could represent a nation whose name he sought not to disclose. Ellicott (page cited) believes this psalm may reflect the conditions of some of the Jews in the Persian Empire. Others had to deal with a nation, or tribes within a nation, who sought to destroy the Jews—such as we find in the history of Esther. Some believe it relates to the Jews who made the return but had to deal with the Samaritans, who sought to destroy them. That there were national implications is underscored in the following statement:

I am for peace,
but when I speak,
They are for war (v. 7).

What we do know about the author is that he was in distress and that he trusted in God:

In my trouble
I cried to the Lord,
And He answered me (v. 1).

We also know that this psalm was intended to be a prayer for God to deal with the wicked:

Deliver my soul, O Lord,
from lying lips,
From a deceitful tongue.
What shall be given to you,
and what more
shall be done to you,
You deceitful tongue?
Sharp arrows of the warrior,
With the burning coals
of the broom tree (vv. 2-4).

These words have influenced some writers to believe the setting would be among the Samaritans because of their constant complaints to the Persian Empire about the returned Jews.

Psalm 121

The internal evidence suggests that the pilgrims may have sung this song as they first caught sight of the mountains surrounding Jerusalem.

I will lift up my eyes
to the mountains;
From whence shall my help come?
My help comes from the Lord,
Who made heaven and earth (vv. 1, 2).

This is an affirmation that God is the ultimate source of their help. The mountains may have afforded some protection, but the Babylonians had broken through anyway. Only

God can bring security. The people were resolved to trust in God by expressing their confidence in Him to keep them:

He will not allow
your foot to slip;
He who keeps you
will not slumber.
Behold, He who keeps Israel
Will neither slumber
nor sleep (vv. 3, 4).

They were confident that God would stay awake and guard them while they slept. The next verses express the confidence of His care during the day:

The Lord is your keeper;
The Lord is your shade
on your right hand.
The sun will not
smite you by day,
Nor the moon by night.
The Lord will protect you
from all evil;
He will keep your soul.
The Lord will guard
your going out
and your coming in
From this time forth
and forever (vv. 5-8).

The tired pilgrim is ready to walk again after such promises have been sung. All of us have experienced the exhilaration of tired bodies when the mind and soul have been renewed.

Psalm 122

The pilgrims may have sung this song as they neared the gates of the Temple, within the walls of the city of Jerusalem. The opening verses reveal the joy of those who participate with the throng moving toward God's house. From the internal evidence it may well have been written during the time of the first Temple, when Jerusalem was in its glory.

I was glad when
they said to me,
"Let us go to
the house of the Lord."
Our feet are standing
Within your gates,
O Jerusalem (vv. 1, 2).

For those who have been there, it is easy to imagine the feeling those two verses brought to the worshipers. Having arrived, we see their attention turn to the holy government of the City of God.

Jerusalem, that is built
As a city that
is compact together (v. 3).

For there thrones
were set for judgment,
The thrones of
the house of David (v. 5).

The closing verses (6-9) constitute a prayer for the peace and prosperity of Israel:

Pray for the peace of Jerusalem:
"May they prosper who love you.

May peace be within your walls,
And prosperity within your palaces" (vv. 6, 7).

For the sake of the house
of the Lord our God
I will seek your good (v. 9).

PSALM 123

To Thee I lift up my eyes,
O Thou who art
enthroned in the heavens!
Behold, as the eyes of servants
look to the hand of their master,
As the eyes of a maid
to the hand of her mistress;
So our eyes look
to the Lord our God,
Until He shall be
gracious to us (vv. 1, 2).

This song seems to come from the Temple. With only four verses, this composition is divided equally into two verses each. In the first half, the worshiper looks to God as the eyes of a servant looks to the hand of his master; he expects deliverance for those who have received contempt and ridicule from the proud and the arrogant. The internal evidence is clear: This was not written when pilgrims made peaceful journeys to the house of the Lord during the reign of Solomon to worship in the first Temple.

Be gracious to us, O Lord,
be gracious to us;
For we are greatly filled

with contempt.
Our soul is greatly filled
With the scoffing of
those who are at ease,
And with the contempt
of the proud (vv. 3, 4).

It is almost certain that this psalm was written after the return from captivity, when the Samaritans did all they could to disrupt their worship, even writing to the Persian government and saying that the Jews were not loyal citizens. In Ezra 5, we are told that Tattenai, governor of the Trans-Euphrates, wrote to King Darius describing how the Jews were rebuilding the Temple. They had tried to find out the names of those involved, but could not. Ezra 6 contains the answer of the king of Persia that in the first year of King Cyrus, such authority had been given them: "Let the temple be rebuilt as a place to present sacrifices, and let its foundations be laid" (6:3, *NIV*). The Samaritans tried to disrupt the building process with many other accusations.

Psalm 124

"Had it not been the Lord
who was on our side,"
Let Israel now say,
"Had it not been the Lord
who was on our side,
When men rose up against us;
Then they would have
swallowed us alive,
When their anger was
kindled against us;

Then the waters
would have engulfed us,
The stream would have
swept over our soul;
Then the raging waters
would have
swept over our soul" (vv. 1-5).

This is obviously a hymn of praise to God for deliverance in time of danger, both individually and nationally. It was titled to David by a scribe who believed himself to be helpful, but internal evidence does not seem to bear this out. Clarke[6] points out that this inscription is not present in the Greek Septuagint or the Latin Vulgate. It is also missing in many other ancient manuscripts.

Blessed be the Lord,
Who has not given us
to be torn by their teeth. . . .
The snare is broken and
we have escaped.
Our help is in
the name of the Lord,
Who made heaven and earth (vv. 6-8).

Thus the author ends as he began, by saying they were facing danger from which they could not possibly escape—had it not been for the Lord who protected them.

Psalm 125

Those who trust in the Lord
Are as Mount Zion,

which cannot be moved,
but abides forever.
As the mountains
surround Jerusalem,
So the Lord
surrounds His people
From this time forth
and forever (vv. 1, 2).

Halley[7] identifies this as a hymn of trust, and adds: "As the mountains are round about Jerusalem, so God is round about his people." He has well caught the theme, for the psalmist begins by saying, "Those who trust in the Lord are as Mount Zion." The short psalm ends with a prayer for the godly but reveals the evil lot of the wicked.

For the scepter of the wickedness
Shall not rest upon
the land of the righteous;
That the righteous
may not put forth
their hands to do wrong.
Do good, O Lord,
to those who are good,
And to those who are
upright in their hearts.
But as for those
who turn aside
to their crooked ways,
The Lord will lead them away
with the doers of iniquity.
Peace be upon Israel (vv. 3-5).

The Jews were convinced that God would not allow the heathen to control the land given to the Israelites, including the Holy City of Zion.

Psalm 126

There is little doubt about the historical setting of this psalm.

When the Lord brought back
the captive ones to Zion,
We were like those who dream (v. 1).

After 70 years in Babylon, the captives found themselves on the 1,000-mile journey back to their homeland. Many who journeyed had not been born when Jerusalem was destroyed. They knew only what their parents had described to them of the glory of what had once been Jerusalem. Others who did return, at an old age and with feeble limbs, were overcome with emotion and felt as if they were sleepwalking.

Then our mouth was
filled with laughter,
And our tongue
with joyful shouting . . . (v. 2).

Even to be among the ruins restored the hope that God had indeed not forgotten them. They believed that God would cause them to see a Temple rebuilt on the site of the first Temple built by Solomon. One can only imagine the emotion that engulfed them as they stumbled into what had once been Zion, the city of God.

The Lord has done
great things for us;

We are glad.
Restore our captivity, O Lord,
As the streams in the South (vv. 3, 4).

The last two verses of this song have become a promise for all who have felt the wrath of the world, but who still serve God:

Those who sow in tears
shall reap with joyful shouting.
He who goes to and fro weeping,
carrying his bag of seed,
Shall indeed come again
with a shout of joy,
bringing his sheaves with him (vv. 5, 6).

Where the Spirit of God is, there is eternal optimism.

Psalm 127

Both the *New American Standard Bible* and the *New International Version* carry in the title the words "of Solomon." Clarke[8] confirms that the Hebrew, Chaldee, and the Vulgate all attribute the song to Solomon. However, this inscription is missing in the Septuagint, Aethioptc [Ethiopic], Arabic and Anglo-Saxon texts. (Note: *Ethiopic* is the modern spelling having to do with Ethiopia. The Latin form is used by Clarke and so appears in this text. A compromise may be to include the modern spelling as I have done.) These translations do not carry an author but simply list it as "A Psalm of Degrees." This brings him to conjecture that it was most likely composed for the building of the second Temple by a prophet at the time of Nehemiah. Ellicott[9] says that "of Solomon" is not the proper way of presenting

Solomon's authorship. This would normally have been read "by Solomon." Perhaps the prophet who wrote the psalm dedicated it to Solomon because of its theme of building. Certainly the author had in mind building of many types.

Unless the Lord builds the house,
They labor in vain who build it (v. 1a).

This could have reference to the Temple or to the walls of the city.

Unless the Lord guards the city,
The watchman keeps awake in vain (v. 1b).

In fact, he seems to apply this principle to all of life's endeavors:

It is vain for you to rise up early,
To retire late,
To eat of the bread
of painful labors;
For He gives to His beloved
even in his sleep (v. 2).

In the latter part of the psalm, he extols the blessings of building a home:

Behold, children are a gift
of the Lord;
The fruit of a womb
is a reward.
Like arrows in
the hand of a warrior,
So are the children
of one's youth.

How blessed is the man
whose quiver is full of them;
They shall not be ashamed,
When they speak
with their enemies
in the gate (vv. 3-5).

Psalm 128

Psalm 128 sounds like a continued theme from 127 in that it also deals with home building. In the previous psalm, the poet pictures the man who fears the Lord with a large number of sons, meeting the enemy at the gate and turning them away. For the time setting of that psalm, this would be the strongest protection one could have.

In this next psalm, we see the same theme. The man who trusts God will have a godly family, who will bless him all his life.

How blessed is everyone
who fears the Lord,
Who walks in His ways.
When you shall eat of
the fruit of your hands,
You will be happy
and it will be
well with you (vv. 1, 2).

Then, in verses 3 and 4, we see this same man from Psalm 127 sitting at supper. Instead of the sons meeting the enemy at the gates, the family is seated about the supper table, enjoying the blessings of God and the joy of family fellowship.

Your wife shall be
like a fruitful vine,
Within your house,
Your children
like olive plants
Around your table.
Behold, for thus shall
the man be blessed
Who fears the Lord (vv. 3, 4).

The olive is often used as a sign of fruitfulness. The man who owns several olive trees is a man with a substantial income. The final verses pronounce God's blessings upon the man who serves Him:

The Lord bless
you from Zion,
And may you see
the prosperity of Jerusalem
all the days of your life.
Indeed, may you see
your children's children.
Peace be upon Israel! (vv. 5, 6).

PSALM 129

Here, the singers pause to invoke God's recognition of the hardships through which they have passed:

"Many times they have persecuted
me from my youth up,"
Let Israel now say,
"Many times they have persecuted

me from my youth up;
Yet they have not
prevailed against me" (vv. 1, 2).

The phrase "from my youth up" is probably meant to recall the sufferings in Egypt, as well as the Babylonian Captivity, and speaks of a nation rather than an individual. The psalm is certainly a product of post-captive Israel, written after the return to Jerusalem.

Verses 5 and 6 describe the desired fate of those who persecuted them:

May all who hate Zion,
Be put to shame
and turned backward,
Let them be like
grass upon the housetops,
Which withers
before it grows up (vv. 5, 6).

It is obvious that Israel has not yet been returned to her original glory—nor will she, until the Son of David is put on the eternal throne. The focus of the psalm is backward rather than forward.

Psalm 130

This song has no title other than "A Song of Ascents." There is no name associated with the composition in any of the versions. Because of its theme, it is generally placed with what is called the Penitential Psalms. From its internal evidence, it appears to have been composed during the Captivity. Because of the voice of the prophets, the Israelites in captivity had come to realize that what they were suffering was due to their own sins. It was not God who had let them down. But because they had turned away from Him, they had seen Jerusalem and the Temple destroyed and they had gone into Babylonian captivity.

This psalm is a lament of Israel for its sins and a confession of God's mercy and forgiveness. Few, if any, psalms communicate the understanding of forgiveness found in the New Testament as this one:

If Thou, Lord,
shouldst mark iniquities,
O Lord, who could stand?
But there is
forgiveness with Thee,
That Thou mayest be feared (vv. 3, 4).

Verse 7 gives Israel ample reason to trust in the Lord:

O Israel, hope in the Lord;
For with the Lord
there is lovingkindness,
And with Him
is abundant redemption.

Certainly the author must have been a prophet with a full grasp of God's love and redemption. As a nation, Israel had not made such a confession. The final words of this psalm in verse 8 reveal hope and assurance in God:

And He will redeem Israel
From all his iniquities.

What greater promise in all the Old Testament could be found? No wonder it was sung by every Israelite on the way up to the Temple. This composition may well have been written while Israel was still in captivity in Babylon, from what we can discover from the internal evidence. But how appropriate that it was included in the Songs of Ascents.

PSALM 131

This song is ascribed to David in the *New American Standard Bible* and the *New International Version* and is supported by Clarke[10] and others. There are other theories, but none throw special light on the meaning of this psalm. In verses 1 and 2, the psalmist expresses the humbleness that we expect of David when standing before the Lord:

O Lord, my heart is not proud,
nor my eyes haughty;
Nor do I involve
myself in great matters,
Or in things
too difficult for me.
Surely I have composed
and quieted my soul;
Like a weaned child
rests against his mother,
My soul is like
a weaned child within me.

This confession is followed with a hope for all Israel and a plea for their submission to God:

O Israel, hope in the Lord
From this time forth
and forever (v. 3).

Psalm 132

Concerning this psalm, there can be little doubt about its purpose and theme. It is a poetical recounting of God's promise to David concerning his selection of Zion and the establishment of an eternal throne. There is little unanimity of thought concerning its authorship. Some have chosen David, but there is little evidence to support his authorship because the writer is speaking of God's promise to David in the past tense. There is more evidence that points to Solomon, since a part of his prayer is included when the first Temple was dedicated. In fact, verses 8-10 of this psalm are exactly the same as 2 Chronicles 6:41, 42:

Arise, O Lord, to Thy resting place;
Thou and the ark of Thy strength.
Let Thy priests be
clothed with righteousness;
And let Thy godly ones
sing for joy.
For the sake of
David Thy servant,
Do not turn away
the face of Thine anointed (vv. 8-10).

It was not unusual for sections from history to be copied in the psalms when it fit the purpose of the author.

In the absence of any title, it is likely that the song was composed at the dedication of the new Temple after the return from captivity. The author calls to witness the promise God made to both David and Solomon when Zion was established as God's earthly resting place. The internal evidence bears this out more than any relation to the first Temple.

The writer begins with an appeal to God concerning the hardships of David.

Remember, O Lord,
on David's behalf,
All his affliction;
How he swore to the Lord,
And vowed to the Mighty One of Jacob,
"Surely I will not enter my house,
Nor lie on my bed;
I will not give sleep to my eyes,
Or slumber to my eyelids;
Until I find a place for the Lord,
A dwelling place for
the Mighty One of Jacob" (vv. 1-5).

This appeal would certainly not be appropriate for a Davidic authorship. The next two verses recount the history of the ark when it was discovered in the house of Kirjath-jearim. It may be a continuation of David's oath before the Lord.

Behold, we heard of
it in Ephrathah;
We found it in
the field of Jaar.
Let us go into
His dwelling place;
Let us worship
at His footstool (vv. 6, 7).

This account is followed by verses 8-10 and the parallel passage from 2 Chronicles 6:41, 42, quoted earlier. The following two verses are perhaps the most significant in the psalm, in light of what happened to the Temple and the subsequent captivity of the people:

The Lord has sworn to David,
A truth from which
He will not turn back;
"Of the fruit of your body
I will set upon your throne.
"If your sons
will keep My covenant,
And My testimony
which I teach them,
Their sons also
shall sit upon
your throne forever" (vv. 11, 12).

Note carefully the promise made to David. The one son, Solomon, did occupy the throne of David. The unconditional promise of verse 11 was fulfilled as promised. In verse 12, however, we find a promise conditioned upon keeping the covenant. The prophets, especially Ezekiel and Daniel, had disclosed to the people how their sins had brought about the destruction of Jerusalem and the Temple. That falling away began in the height of Solomon's reign, because of his own idolatry.

The kingdom was torn away from the first son of Solomon, Rehoboam, when Jeroboam arose and broke away the 10 tribes from the house of David. Even though Rehoboam still occupied the throne of David, it no longer held its former glory. The 10 tribes were never restored, and David's kingdom (Judah) was finally overrun by Babylon. Then the prophets began to cry more and more for God to raise up a son to sit on the throne. These prophecies were, of course, fulfilled in Christ. The closing verses reiterate the promise to David and the glory that would come to Zion.

For the Lord has chosen Zion;
He has desired it for His habitation.
"This is My resting place forever;
Here I will dwell,
for I have desired it.
"I will abundantly bless her provision;
I will satisfy her needy with bread.
"Her priests also
I will clothe with salvation;
And her godly ones
will sing aloud for joy" (vv. 13-16).

A solemn assurance is given by God that Zion will forever be His dwelling place. Just as the Israelites needed to be reminded of this truth, Christians today look forward to the same reality. When He promised abundant food for His people, He did not forget the poor. We should be careful to follow His example. As God blesses us, we have the obligation—even more so the privilege—to bless others.

"There I will cause
the horn of David
to spring forth;
I have prepared
a lamp for Mine anointed.
"His enemies
I will clothe with shame;
But upon himself
his crown shall shine" (vv. 17, 18).

The horn that is to grow for David, and the glorious crown reserved for him, has strong implications for the Messiah.

Note that here is the answer to the prayer of Solomon at the dedication of the Temple in 2 Chronicles:

"Now therefore arise, O Lord God,
to Thy resting place,
Thou and the ark of Thy might;
let Thy priests, O Lord God,
be clothed with salvation,
and let Thy godly ones
rejoice in what is good.
"O Lord God, do not turn away
the face of Thine anointed . . ." (6:41, 42).

PSALM 133

This short psalm is ascribed to David in the Hebrew, Syriac and the Vulgate, but this title is omitted in the Septuagint, Aethiopic [Ethiopic], Arabic and Anglo-Saxon versions, according to Clarke[11]. But the theme is not in question. It is a psalm of unity of a brotherhood, primarily the brotherhood of the priesthood, because of the anointing pictured. But it is equally precious for the family, the Christian brotherhood of a local church, or the body of Christ in general.

Behold, how good and how pleasant it is
For brothers to dwell together in unity!
It is like the precious oil upon the head,
Coming down upon the beard,
Even Aaron's beard,
Coming down upon
the edge of his robes (vv. 1, 2).

The composition of the holy anointing oil is described in Exodus 30:23, 24. It was composed of liquid myrrh, fragrant cinnamon, fragrant cane, cassia and olive oil. The fragrance must have been especially treasured by those who had been recipients of this holy anointing. Psalm 133:3 compares it to the visual beauty described in verse 2:

It is like the dew of Hermon,
Coming down upon
the mountains of Zion;
For there the Lord
commanded the blessing—
life forever (v. 3).

The summit of Mount Hermon is covered with snow the year round. It is the source of the Jordan, which flows through Israel and distributes its benefits. The poet was describing the continuous blessings upon God's people, which flowed out to bless all the earth about them.

Psalm 134

The last of the Songs of Ascents elevates the brotherhood of the priests and Levites, especially those who had the responsibility of ministering by night in the sanctuary. Note verses 1 and 2:

Behold, bless the Lord,
all servants of the Lord,
Who serve by night
in the house of the Lord!
Lift up your hands to the sanctuary,
And bless the Lord.

Verse 3 seems to be the prayer for the high priest who is going to his rest, but may be equally applicable to all who serve the Lord:

> *May the Lord bless you from Zion,*
> *He who made heaven and earth.*

6

Prayers of Penitence

There may be many penitential elements in the Psalms, but only the following seven are recognized as having penitence as their primary theme: 6, 25, 32, 38, 51, 102, and 142. The collectors of the Book of Psalms did not group the psalms with the same themes together as modern songbooks do. They were more interested in collection by authors.

Psalm 6

This psalm of David expresses sorrow of many kinds. In verses 1-3, David cries out for healing because of his sin:

O Lord, do not rebuke me in your anger
or discipline me in your wrath.
Be merciful to me, Lord,
for I am faint;
O Lord, heal me,
for my bones are in agony.

My soul is in anguish.
How long, O Lord, how long?

David does not reveal the reason for his anguish because he knew that God understood his prayer to Him. In his anguish, David admits that he deserves the sickness, but he also believes that God will deliver. Most writers believe this psalm, like others, refers to the time when he sinned with Bathsheba. However, it should not be assumed that this was the only time when David needed to cry out to God.

In verses 4 and 5, David cries out for deliverance. He knows that if he is delivered, it will be because of God's love, not his own worthiness. He argues that he will be worth more to God alive than dead.

Turn, O Lord, and deliver me;
save me because of your unfailing love.
No one remembers you when he is dead.
Who praises you from the grave?

Only those who have known deep conviction to the point of tears and who fear that God may give them up to death can understand verses 6 and 7:

I am worn out from groaning;
all night long I flood my bed with weeping
and drench my couch with tears.
My eyes grow weak with sorrow;
they fail because of all my foes.

In addition to being sorrowful before God, David had to deal with the fact that many in his kingdom had turned away from him. This may be an unknown sorrow that had to do with his judgment in kingdom matters. Every child of God should be heartened by these closing verses of assurance:

Away from me, all you who do evil,
for the Lord has heard my weeping.
The Lord has heard my cry for mercy;
the Lord accepts my prayer.
All my enemies will be ashamed and dismayed;
they will turn back in sudden disgrace (vv. 8-10).

There would be no point in including a psalm that depicted only weeping. David knew how to repent and receive the joy of forgiveness in whatever problem he brought to God.

Psalm 25

In this psalm, David's soul is deeply distressed because of his sins and his troubles. We can relate to this need for forgiveness for our sins and deliverance from our trouble. For this reason, we can profit from reading this prayer of a man oppressed by sin and trouble. We looked at this psalm when discussing the alphabetical grouping, but it also has a special place in the penitential psalms.

This prayer begins with a statement of trust in the Lord, while some of the penitential psalms begin with a hopelessness because of sin. Here David expresses a strong trust:

To you, O Lord, I lift up my soul;
in you I trust, O my God (vv. 1, 2a).

Next, David suggests that he needs deliverance from his enemies rather than his individual sin. Later in the psalm he addresses his sins.

Do not let me be put to shame,
nor let my enemies triumph over me.
No one whose hope is in you
will ever be put to shame,
but they will be put to shame
who are treacherous
without excuse (vv. 2b, 3).

In a way that is clearly Davidic, he turns again to express hope in God. How often in trouble we dwell on our troubles, even in prayer. David turns to God constantly as his hope and security.

Show me your ways, O Lord,
teach me your paths;
guide me in your truth and teach me,
for you are God my Savior,
and my hope is in you all day long (vv. 4, 5).

When he confesses his sin, he is referring to his youth rather than a recent fall. In this he differs from most other psalms of penitence:

Remember, O Lord, your great mercy and love,
for they are from of old.
Remember not the sins of my youth
and my rebellious ways;
According to your love remember me,
for you are good, O Lord (vv. 6, 7).

David even mentions his rebellious ways in his youth, of which we know nothing but good. Even in the best of men, the old nature is present even if it is not known publicly. But he does not dwell upon his early sins because he is forgiven. He rather turns quickly to praising the Lord for his goodness to men.

> *Good and upright is the Lord;*
> *therefore he instructs sinners in his ways.*
> *He guides the humble in what is right*
> *and teaches them his way.*
> *All the ways of the Lord are loving and faithful*
> *for those who keep*
> *the demands of his covenant* (vv. 8-10).

Here David refers to himself as humble in contrast to what he referred to earlier as his rebellious ways. David regards himself now to be on the right path. But immediately he moves from the sins of his youth to what he calls his great sin:

> *For the sake of your name, O Lord,*
> *forgive my iniquity, though it is great* (v. 11).

His troubles appear again in verses 16–18 as he continues to cry out to God:

> *Turn to me and be gracious to me,*
> *for I am lonely and afflicted.*
> *The troubles of my heart have multiplied;*
> *free me from my anguish.*
> *Look upon my affliction and my distress*
> *and take away all my sins.*

Note the strong words that indicate his present trouble: *lonely, afflicted, anguished* and *distressed.* All of these could be remedied if God would remove the guilt of his sin. In verses 20 and 22, David's writing indicates that his own troubles are also the troubles of all Israel:

Guard my life and rescue me;
let me not be put to shame.
Redeem Israel, O God,
from all their troubles!

Some believe that the entire psalm may be a confession on Israel's behalf. Most likely it is David's personal anguish that parallels Israel's rebellion in the early days before turning to God.

PSALM 32

We looked at this prayer when we dealt with the didactic psalms because it teaches the benefit of having sins forgiven. In this section we will address more particularly the cry for forgiveness on the part of David. There is little doubt that here David is dealing with his sin with Bathsheba, but there is a difference of opinion as to what stage it appears. Some think it was the conviction of his heart before the sin was made public. Others argue that it was written after his great confession in Psalm 51 when his heart had been quieted by God's forgiveness. In either case, it is a companion of the great prayer of repentance in Psalm 51.

It is said that Augustine was so moved by this great psalm that he often read it with weeping and, before his death, had it written on his wall so that he could read it from his deathbed.[1] This was not only because of the confession in verses 1-6, but also because of verses 7-11, where David rejoices in the great comfort of a man whose sins were forgiven.

When I kept silent,
my bones wasted away
through my groaning all day long.

For day and night
your hand was heavy upon me;
my strength was sapped
as in the heat of summer.
Selah (vv. 3, 4).

Note the phrases that indicate that David was completely overcome by his guilt: wasted away, groaning day and night, his strength was sapped as one with heat exhaustion.

Then I acknowledged my sin to you
and did not cover up my iniquity.
I said, "I will confess
my transgressions to the Lord"—
and you forgave the guilt of my sin.
Selah (v. 5).

The result of true repentance is true forgiveness. David had said in verse 1:

Blessed is he whose
transgressions are forgiven,
whose sins are covered.

Then, in verse 10, he sums up both his personal testimony and his personal observations:

Many are the woes of the wicked,
but the Lord's unfailing love
surrounds the man who trusts in him.

Psalm 38

This prayer for mercy is assigned to David. Strangely the Septuagint carries the title "A Psalm of David for a

Commemoration of the Sabbath." Clarke[2] points out that there is no mention of the Sabbath in it. Rather, he identifies it as a deeply penitential psalm, and that is its primary theme. There is no explanation as to how this title of the Sabbath became attached.

The internal evidence does not seem to connect David's sin with Bathsheba and the resulting repentance, although the psalm certainly seems to embody the same kind of sorrow and acknowledgment of sin found in Psalm 51.

> *O Lord, do not rebuke me in your anger*
> *or discipline me in your wrath* (Psalm 38:1).

David does not argue here that God would not be justified by meeting out such discipline, but rather he pleads for mercy as he expresses his anguish.

> *For your arrows have pierced me,*
> *and your hand has come down upon me.*
> *Because of your wrath*
> *there is no health in my body;*
> *my bones have no soundness*
> *because of my sin.*
> *My guilt has overwhelmed me*
> *like a burden too heavy to bear* (vv. 2-4).

In typical Davidic fashion, the writer takes the blame to himself and brings his personal guilt to God.

> *My wounds fester and are loathsome*
> *because of my sinful folly* (v. 5).

Halley[3] believes that here David is admitting he is suffering from a disease, which has plagued him because of his sin. This causes his friends to turn away from him. Most of us do not like to think of David suffering from a sexually transmitted disease, but his words certainly speak of this possibility.

> *I am bowed down and brought very low;*
> *all day long I go about mourning.*
> *My back is filled with searing pain;*
> *there is no health in my body.*
> *I am feeble and utterly crushed;*
> *I groan in anguish of heart* (vv. 6-8).

David's body was full of pain and his heart was full of anguish. The "man after God's own heart" was not exempt from suffering. This does not bring any consolation to any of us who suffer because of sin, except to teach us that suffering follows sin and no one is exempt. It is simply a delusion when some think they can become so powerful in the Lord's work that He will overlook their transgressions. Power often makes people feel that they are exempt from God's law, but this is not so. St. Jerome[4] taught that "if any sickness happens to the body, we are to seek for the medicine of the soul."

David is now in greater danger because his sin has made it possible for those who already hated him to take advantage of him and lay traps to destroy him.

> *Those who seek my life set their traps,*
> *those who would harm me talk of my ruin;*
> *all day long they plot deception* (v. 12).

David was so distraught that he was not even able to speak to those who spoke to him. Who can imagine a condition so severe! Worse still, he sees no hope of recovery. In verse 16, he uses the term "when my foot slips" as if that were inevitable. Normally, we would have expected David to have said "*if* my foot slips," but never would we expect him to anticipate certain ruin.

I am like a deaf man,
who cannot hear,
like a mute,
who cannot open his mouth;
I have become like a man
who does not hear,
whose mouth can offer no reply.
I wait for you, O Lord;
you will answer, O Lord my God.
For I said, "Do not let them gloat
or exalt themselves over me
when my foot slips" (vv. 13-16).

David made no excuses. He laid his sin before the Lord with a full confession. Can anyone wonder why he was a man after God's own heart? How unlike many modern believers who simply have no thought about the confession of sin. They dismiss it with the thought that God has already accepted the work of Christ and don't give sin any more thought.

For I am about to fall,
and my pain is ever with me.
I confess my iniquity;
I am troubled by my sin (vv. 17, 18).

Note David's closing words where he exhibits faith, in spite of his failure, because his faith rests in God's mercy:

O Lord, do not forsake me;
be not far from me, O my God.
Come quickly to help me,
O Lord my Savior (vv. 21, 22).

Psalm 51

This is the greatest prayer of repentance ever written. The title says it is "a psalm of David, when the prophet Nathan came to him after David had committed adultery with Bathsheba." Some have doubted the Davidic authorship because of the last two verses. But we will discuss that in due course. No other psalm presents the New Testament concept of repentance and forgiveness as this one does.

Have mercy on me, O God,
according to your unfailing love;
according to your great compassion
blot out my transgressions.
Wash away all my iniquity
and cleanse me from my sin (vv. 1, 2).

Note that this Old Testament passage says nothing about offering 50 bullocks or 100 rams for the sin committed. This might have been what the religious leaders of Jesus' day would have prescribed. But the Holy Spirit, working through the heart of David, revealed to him that forgiveness was not based on such sacrifices. He asks not for just a covering but a cleansing from sin, which certainly is a Christian concept.

For I know my transgressions,
and my sin is always before me (v. 3).

Until confronted by Nathan, David had convinced himself that he had done what any other king would have done. After all, was he not a ruler and did he not make the laws as he saw fit? Had he not taken other wives? But God's messenger had spoken to him on God's behalf, and he now saw clearly what he had chosen to overlook earlier.

Against you, you only, have I sinned
and done what is evil in your sight,
so that you are proved right when you speak
and justified when you judge (v. 4).

These are strange words for a man who has made a clear confession and pleaded for complete cleansing. What about Bathsheba? Had she not willingly come to him at his invitation? And had she not in reality provoked the incident? What about her husband? Had Joab not written to him and told him that Uriah had died in battle and that war takes one as well as another? The human mind is skilled at maintaining its own righteousness. And so he continues by saying he could not help himself.

Surely I was sinful at birth,
sinful from the time
my mother conceived me (v. 5).

But God did not accept that, and David had a flash of spiritual insight.

Surely you desire truth
in the inner parts;
you teach me wisdom
in the inmost place (v. 6).

The Spirit again cleared his heart and mind and caused him to utter the following profound truth:

Cleanse me with hyssop,
and I will be clean;
wash me, and I will be
whiter than snow (v. 7).

Hyssop was a bush used for sprinkling the blood on the mantle and doorpost at the Passover. David understood the blood significance, even though "whiter than snow" was not a concept for his day. The author continues to anticipate the joy of forgiveness.

> *Let me hear joy and gladness;*
> *let the bones you have crushed rejoice.*
> *Hide your face from my sins*
> *and blot out all my iniquity* (vv. 8, 9).

All this has not yet happened, so he continues to implore the Lord to finish the work in his heart.

> *Create in me a pure heart, O God,*
> *and renew a steadfast spirit within me.*
> *Do not cast me from your presence*
> *or take your Holy Spirit from me.*
> *Restore to me the joy of your salvation*
> *and grant me a willing spirit,*
> *to sustain me* (vv. 10-12).

The pure heart for which he asks is one without the sin that has so burdened him. The steadfast spirit would be the ability to maintain a pure heart. Note how clearly he understands the work of the Holy Spirit a thousand years before Pentecost. He asks for the joy of salvation, realizing there is no joy without God's forgiveness. Often we hear people say they have lost their joy without realizing why. His offer to teach transgressors the way of the Lord is found in the next verse:

> *Then I will teach transgressors your ways,*
> *and sinners will turn back to you* (v. 13).

David believes he can still serve the Lord if God will cleanse his heart. He cries out again when he remembers the death of Uriah, which he has caused on the battlefield.

Save me from bloodguilt, O God,
the God who saves me,
and my tongue will sing of your righteousness.
O Lord, open my lips,
and my mouth will declare your praise (vv. 14, 15).

In the next two verses David explains his New Testament concept of forgiveness in contrast to that required in the law of the Old Testament. It is obvious that such a revelation is a part of the work of the Holy Spirit in his heart.

You do not delight in sacrifice,
or I would bring it;
you do not take pleasure in burnt offerings.
The sacrifices of God are a broken spirit;
a broken and contrite heart, O God,
you will not despise (vv. 16, 17).

Some scholars think that the final verses were written by a post-exilic priest and attached to this prayer of David. It would have been attached here because the history of Israel had in some sense duplicated the sin of David. It would also defend the sacrificial system that seems to have been discarded in the last part of David's prayer.

In your good pleasure make Zion prosper;
build up the walls of Jerusalem.
Then there will be righteous sacrifices,
whole burnt offerings to delight you;
then bulls will be offered on your altar (vv. 18, 19).

Others have thought that the entire psalm was non-Davidic because of the obvious timing of these last verses. But not only does the title clearly ascribe the psalm to David but it also describes the historical occasion that precipitated it in 2 Samuel 12.

It is not necessary to conclude that David did not write the last two verses. It may seem strained, but some believe these verses were written by David and fulfilled under Solomon. In either respect, we should not allow the significance of this great psalm to be reduced by whatever happened in these last two verses. It remains the greatest of the psalms of penitence in Scripture.

Psalm 102

Ellicott[5] believes the title to this psalm was added long after its writing: "A prayer of the afflicted, when he is overwhelmed, and poureth out his complaint before the Lord." Because it has neither author nor music indication, it is thought to have been added by some scribe to indicate how it may best be used. It is obvious that it may be used in private devotion, as well as public. Clarke[6] believes that there is sufficient internal evidence to say with surety that the author was in Babylon during the Captivity—probably close to the end of that horrible experience. We will call attention to some of these verses in place, but verses 14-17 are proof that the time of its writing dates from the period of exile. It seems obvious that the writer expressed the distress of a national calamity, as well as a personal distress that resulted from the condition of the nation as a whole. In verses 1-7 the writer gives explicit explanation of his condition:

Hear my prayer, O Lord;
let my cry for help come to you.

Do not hide your face from me
when I am in distress.
Turn your ear to me;
when I call, answer me quickly.
For my days vanish like smoke;
my bones burn like glowing embers.
My heart is blighted
and withered like grass;
I forget to eat my food.
Because of my loud groaning
I am reduced to skin and bones.
I am like a desert owl,
like an owl among the ruins.
I lie awake;
I have become like a bird
alone on a roof (vv. 1-7).

Some of these dramatic descriptions may be considered as overstatements unless you can imagine worshiping God in His tabernacle in Jerusalem, believing that He would always care for His people. Then imagine the armies of Babylon destroying not only Jerusalem but also the very Temple where God dwelled. In doing so, they murdered women and children and killed the armies who tried to defend the city. God seemed to offer no help. Then came the 1,000-mile march to Babylon where many died along the way. Now you wait—40, 50, or maybe 60 years—and you lose all hope of deliverance. But you continue to pray for the release of Israel and the return to Jerusalem. Under these circumstances, this psalm would seem appropriate. In verses 8-11 the writer calls attention to two causes that precipitated his difficulties—his enemies and his belief that God has thrown him aside.

All day long my enemies taunt me;
those who rail against me
use my name as a curse.
For I eat ashes as my food
and mingle my drink with tears
because of your great wrath,
for you have taken me up
and thrown me aside.
My days are like the evening shadow;
I wither away like grass.

In verses 12 and 13 the writer reestablishes his faith in the eternal God. Though man may wither and perish, the eternal God will never fail.

But you, O Lord,
sit enthroned forever;
your renown endures
through all generations.
You will arise
and have compassion on Zion,
for it is time to show favor to her;
the appointed time has come.

It is difficult to determine whether the appointed time was in hope or whether this was written soon after the decree of Cyrus. That Jerusalem had not been rebuilt is obvious here:

For her stones are dear
to your servants;

her very dust moves them to pity.
The nations will fear
the name of the Lord,
all the kings of the earth
will revere your glory.
For the Lord will rebuild Zion
and appear in his glory.
He will respond
to the prayers of the destitute;
he will not despise their plea (vv. 14-17).

It is obvious now that the psalmist has focused his prayer on the future of Israel and her return to Jerusalem, although that has not yet taken place. He has a steadfast confidence that it will take place, though he may not see it.

Let this be written
for a future generation,
that a people not yet created
may praise the Lord:
"The Lord looked down
from his sanctuary on high,
from heaven he viewed the earth,
to hear the groans of the prisoners
and release those
condemned to death" (vv. 18-20).

The psalmist is expecting God to deliver his prisoners who will inhabit the city of Jerusalem.

So the name of the Lord
will be declared in Zion

and his praise in Jerusalem
when the peoples and the kingdoms
assemble to worship the Lord (vv. 21, 22).

Then the writer returns to his personal complaint.

In the course of my life
he broke my strength;
he cut short my days.
So I said:
"Do not take me away, O my God,
in the midst of my days;
your years go on
through all generations" (vv. 23, 24).

His plea is to live to see the restoration of Jerusalem. But hope is still dim. He acknowledges God as creator of all things and believes God could fulfill his desire, although He probably will not.

"In the beginning
you laid the foundations of the earth,
and the heavens are the work of your hands.
They will perish, but you remain;
they will all wear out like a garment.
Like clothing you will change them
and they will be discarded.
But you remain the same,
and your years will never end" (vv. 25-27).

In closing, the writer moves to a theme of assurance that not only will God live, but He will also establish His people again.

"The children of your servants
will live in your presence;
their descendants will
be established before you" (v. 28).

How great is the faith of a man who has endured so much but still believes God will deliver His own! What a contrast this is to some of us whose faith is shaken because God does not heal us immediately of the common cold.

Psalm 142

It is thought by some scholars that this psalm was written by David when he was being pursued by his son Absalom (2 Samuel 17; 18). If so, that would be a time of general unrest in his kingdom and a special time of unrest for him personally. Not only was Absalom seeking David's life, but he was also joined by many powerful men in the kingdom, including one of David's personal advisers, Ahithophel. Absalom's plan was to kill his father and those who had fled with him across the Jordan and take the throne. The Scripture indicates that much time had been spent in laying the plan and, at this point, it was working. We have to understand the complete upheaval in David's kingdom to understand the cry of this psalm.

I cry aloud to the Lord;
I lift up my voice to the Lord for mercy.
I pour out my complaint before him;
before him I tell my trouble (vv. 1, 2).

David knew enough to realize that if God did not help him, he was helpless. The small number of men who went with him from the Royal Court were no match for those who had been gathered in stealth by Absalom. Also, when David vacated the throne, Absalom could call the army to fight for him. Given the unrest, there is no doubt that a large number of others who were dissatisfied would have responded.

When my spirit grows faint within me,
it is you who know my way.
In the path where I walk
men have hidden a snare for me.
Look to my right and see;
no one is concerned for me.
I have no refuge;
no one cares for my life (vv. 3, 4).

David was not exaggerating. Unless God came to his rescue, there could be no help. The Bathsheba incident had turned many against him. When Absalom raped his half-sister, David banished him from his presence. This gave him plenty of time and opportunity to plot against his father and to offer men close to David special honor in the kingdom of Absalom. David saw clearly what was happening, but he could not turn the tide.

I cry to you, O Lord;
I say "You are my refuge,
my portion in the land of the living."
Listen to my cry,
for I am in desperate need;
rescue me from those who pursue me,
for they are too strong for me (vv. 5, 6).

Not only were they too strong for David, but now David was also too weak for them. He had given orders that his son Absalom should not be killed. The king had lost his ability to lead, and the people knew it. Had not Joab disobeyed the king's orders and killed Absalom, the reign of David would have ended in the wilderness, and Absalom would have captured the throne with little or no resistance from the people.

Set me free from my prison,
that I may praise your name.
Then the righteous will gather about me
because of your goodness to me (v. 7).

God answered David's prayer and returned him to the throne. The damage had already been done in the eyes of the people. When David was on his deathbed, another son, Adonijah, gathered the people together to make himself king. Had it not been for the prophet Nathan, David would not have been able to place Solomon on the throne. In this rebellion, even Joab, the captain of the hosts of Israel, had joined with Adonijah. When Nathan and Bathsheba came to David with the news, David sent Nathan to declare Solomon king. But for now, God had answered the prayer of David and had set him free from the prison in which he had entrapped himself. Otherwise, David would have died in the wilderness. This was the answer to the prayer of verse 7.

7 Prayers of Supplication

The term *supplication* is used in the Book of Psalms to identify a formal request to God for a special need or desire. This can be in the form of a personal request or a request for others or an entire nation.

In this chapter we will look at particular prayers addressed to God, identify their location and purpose and, when it can be determined, discuss the historical setting. If possible, the person making the request will be identified. However, there are many requests in the psalms where no title is given and no author identified. In these cases, the person, or the time setting and a likely author, will be identified from the internal support of the Scriptures.

These elements will be researched in the following psalms: 3-5, 13, 43, 44, 54, 70, 86, 88, 140 and 141. Because of the nature of the Book of Psalms, some of these elements may have been addressed under a different classification and therefore may not be discussed in this section.

PSALM 3

Most scholars agree that this psalm of David was written when he fled from his son Absalom. The account in 2 Samuel 15 describes how David was driven from the throne and how Absalom was seeking his life so that he would have no contender for the throne. Clarke[1] suggests it was probably written as David left Jerusalem in sackcloth and passed by the Mount of Olives. There is nothing in the internal evidence to counter this description and much to support it. The fact that it does not contain the name of Absalom is because David tended to blame others for the rebellion. The fact that he gave orders to spare his son suggests that he thought (or wanted to think) that his son was simply a pawn for those who wanted to take his throne and his life.

O Lord, how my adversaries have increased!
Many are rising up against me (v. 1).

The opening verse indicates that David regarded this as a general rebellion and not simply his son with a few followers.

Many are saying of my soul,
"There is no deliverance
for him in God." Selah (v. 2).

The uprising did not seem to be a march of all 12 tribes against Jerusalem, but it did include a substantial number of leading administrators with thousands who wanted to overthrow David. The number was only 200 at first, but they included a counselor of David named Ahithophel. They sent messengers throughout the land that Absalom would be declared king.

The king knew that the few who followed him indicated

that the nation of Israel in general would not come to his defense. Furthermore, some of his closest friends told him that the hearts of the people were no longer with him but with Absalom (2 Samuel 15:13). We have alluded to the fact that David's affair with Bathsheba had eroded his support in Israel. The word *Selah* included in Psalm 3:2 is thought to mean "pause and reflect." In some cases the pause is to reflect on the goodness of God. Here the pause is a dramatic one to show the awful plight of David. But verses 3 and 4 underscore the fact that in the face of what seemed to be impossible circumstances, David expected God to hear his supplication and deliver him:

But Thou, O Lord,
art a shield about me,
My glory, and the One
who lifts my head.
I was crying to the Lord
with my voice,
And He answered me
from His holy mountain.
Selah.

David's confidence in the Lord was equal to all the problems he faced. For this reason, the singers again placed "Selah" to indicate that the dire plight in which David found himself was not going to overwhelm him—his petition to God would be answered. The "holy mountain" to which he alludes was Jerusalem, which Israel regarded as God's dwelling place on earth.

I lay down and slept;
I awoke,

for the Lord sustains me.
I will not be afraid of
ten thousands of people
Who have set themselves
against me round about (vv. 5, 6).

Absalom had laid his plan well. David knew that his small group had no military might against those who surrounded him, which he estimated as tens of thousands. This was a general way of saying at least 20,000, but he thought it could be many more than that. Since David was a warrior, he would not be expected to exaggerate the number. However, in this case, David probably could not make a reasonable estimate. In the face of such circumstances, he could still sleep through the night and awake refreshed in the knowledge that God had protected him.

We must admit that such faith has eluded us on many occasions, which in reality were not nearly so dire. How many nights' sleep have we lost only to wake in the morning and find the threat was not even present.

Arise, O Lord;
save me, O my God!
For thou hast smitten
all my enemies
on the cheek;
Thou hast shattered
the teeth of the wicked (v. 7).

This petition was answered when Joab killed Absalom and David was saved. His heart then turns from what had seemed to be his certain peril . . . and he prayed for his people.

Salvation belongs to the Lord;
Thy blessing be upon
Thy people! Selah (v. 8).

PSALM 4

This psalm of David includes in its title "For the choir director," a phrase that appears in 55 psalms with some change in the preposition. According to Ellicott[2] the term *Neginoth* (which is also a part of the title in the KJV) means literally "to touch the strings" and is used in six psalms. Halley[3] says this is "An Evening Prayer" (see vv. 7, 8).

The theme of Psalm 4 is somewhat similar to that of Psalm 3, although the distress does not seem so urgent. Clarke[4] also regards it as an evening hymn and thought it was sung by David and his men while they were fleeing from Absalom. At that time, David had enough enemies. Whether or not this refers to the same problem as chapter 3 is not certain.

Answer me when I call,
O God of my righteousness!
Thou hast relieved me
in my distress;
Be gracious to me
and hear my prayer (v. 1).

David asks for an answer before he makes his prayer. This adds to the urgency of the request. He then addresses those who seek to destroy him.

O sons of men,
how long will my honor

become a reproach?
How long will you love
what is worthless
and aim at deception? Selah (v. 2).

David is still speaking to God, but he draws a distinction between himself and those who seek to destroy him.

But know that the Lord has set apart
the godly man for Himself;
The Lord hears when I call to Him (v. 3).

David assures himself, and his enemies who cannot hear him, that there is a difference between the godly and the ungodly and that he belongs in the former group. For this reason, God will hear him and deliver him.

Tremble, and do not sin;
Meditate in your heart
upon your bed,
and be still. Selah.
Offer the sacrifices
of righteousness,
And trust in the Lord (vv. 4, 5).

David seems to be addressing others, but he may indeed be rehearsing his own plea.

Many are saying,
"Who will show us any good?"
Lift up the light
of Thy countenance
upon us, O Lord! (v. 6).

His argument is that although others may see no good in serving God, he does.

Thou hast put gladness in my heart,
More than when their grain
and new wine abound.
In peace I will both lie down and sleep,
For Thou alone, O Lord,
Dost make me to dwell in safety (vv. 7, 8).

Then David answers the question his enemies are asking. Yes, there is good and he is receiving it with joy in his heart and grain in his storehouse. Further, he is safe from his enemies.

Psalm 5

This psalm of David is called "A Morning Prayer" by some authors based on the reading in verse 3. The title indicates that the tune is to be played with a flute, as indicated in the *New American Standard Version*. This is suggested by the word *Nehiloth* (KJV), which in the Hebrew refers to a "bored instrument" such as a horn.

Leupold[5] observes that the general tone of Psalm 5 is much like Psalms 3 and 4. The great need expressed here seems to be more general than personal.

Give ear to my words, O Lord,
Consider my groaning.
Heed the sound of my cry for help,
my King and my God,
For to Thee do I pray (vv. 1, 2).

The psalmist expresses his need to the Lord and expects Him to respond. He does indicate it is a cry for help. But unlike the two previous psalms, it could be sung by anyone, on any occasion, because it makes no reference to an immediate danger.

In the morning, O Lord,
Thou wilt hear my voice;
In the morning I will order
my prayer to Thee
and eagerly watch (v. 3).

As any child of God may do today, the writer counts it natural to start the day with prayer and petition and wait for God to respond.

For Thou art not a God
who takes pleasure in wickedness;
No evil dwells with Thee.
The boastful shall not
stand before Thine eyes;
Thou dost hate all
who do iniquity.
Thou dost destroy those
who speak falsehood;
The Lord abhors the man
of bloodshed and deceit (vv. 4-6).

The prayer here is that God will act out His nature. It is worth repeating that the Psalms recognize only two classes of men—the godly and the wicked. Here David distinguishes between God's attitude toward the wicked and, in the next two verses, the godly:

But as for me,
by Thine abundant lovingkindness

I will enter Thy house,
At Thy holy temple I will bow
in reverence for Thee.
O Lord, lead me in Thy righteousness
because of my foes;
Make Thy way straight before me (vv. 7, 8).

These verses are excellent examples of a prayer that could be made by any congregation. Singing this psalm extols God's righteousness and expects Him to make paths straight.

In verses 9 and 10 the psalmist turns to the nature of the wicked and declares God's judgment against them:

There is nothing reliable in what they say;
Their inward part is destruction itself;
Their throat is an open grave;
They flatter with their tongue.
Hold them guilty, O God;
By their own devices let them fall!
In the multitude of their transgressions
thrust them out,
For they are rebellious against Thee.

The petition here is that God will do what He has already determined to do—judge the wicked according to their wickedness. David concludes his morning prayer with a request for the righteous to receive His blessings:

But let all who take refuge
in Thee be glad,
Let them ever sing for joy;
And mayest Thou shelter them,

That those who love Thy name
may exult in Thee.
For it is Thou who dost bless
the righteous man, O Lord,
Thou dost surround him with favor
as with a shield (vv. 11, 12).

David not only prays for himself, but he also prays for all of God's people. It is interesting to note the request for God to spread His protection over His people and not for himself alone. God's favor was being petitioned for all who serve Him.

Psalm 13

This psalm of David is thought by several authors to have been written when David was running from Saul. The song begins with a very intense call to God.

How long, O Lord?
Wilt Thou forget me forever?
How long wilt Thou hide
Thy face from me?
How long shall I take
counsel in my soul,
Having sorrow in my heart
all the day?
How long will my enemy
be exalted over me? (vv. 1, 2).

In rapid succession, David asks questions about his condition that he could not understand. There are times when the struggle of our minds overwhelms us. However, David did not stop there . . . and neither should we. If we are going to ask questions, at least we should ask for answers as he did in the following verses:

Consider and answer me,
O Lord, my God;
Enlighten my eyes,
lest I sleep the sleep of death,
Lest my enemy say,
"I have overcome him,"
Lest my adversaries rejoice
when I am shaken (vv. 3, 4).

It seems that David is asking for his eyes to remain open until he can escape, fearing he would fall asleep and lose his life. However, in the final verses, he claims the promise before he is actually delivered.

But I have trusted
in Thy lovingkindness;
My heart shall rejoice
in Thy salvation.
I will sing to the Lord,
Because He has dealt
bountifully with me (vv. 5, 6).

PSALM 43

This psalm is untitled in our English translations. Clarke[6] says the Syriac version carries this following title: "By David when Jonathan told him that Saul intended to slay him." These titles are not inspired as the text is, but they can be helpful because they are ancient. It is also Clarke's thinking that because of the nature of this psalm, it could have been a part of the preceding psalm. Indeed, he found that in many ancient manuscripts, Psalm 43 is attached to Psalm 42. He believes that for some reason, a division was made at a later date. Such an error could have occurred if the scribe found it necessary to attach part of a long psalm to another manuscript and not make a notation about its continuance. Another scribe could then regard it as a separate work. This would be a possible reason for its lack of title. If this could be established, it would show the psalm to be of the sons of Korah, as is Psalm 42.

Two petitions seem to be contained in the psalm. The first is a request for vindication for the writer, who has been maligned by his enemies.

Vindicate me, O God,
and plead my case
against an ungodly nation;
O deliver me from
the deceitful and unjust man!
For thou art the God of my strength;
why hast Thou rejected me?
Why do I go mourning
because of the oppression
of the enemy? (vv. 1, 2).

As the first request is for vindication, the second is for restoration. In our prayer life we would do well to never just cry to God about what is wrong. Our request for deliverance should be followed with an expression of faith in God to accomplish it.

O send out Thy light and Thy truth,
let them lead me;

Let them bring me to Thy holy hill,
And to Thy dwelling places.
Then will I go to the altar of God,
To God my exceeding joy;
And upon the lyre
I shall praise Thee,
O God, my God (vv. 3, 4).

The closing verse is a refrain that is also found in Psalm 42:5, 11. Since these are the same words and are obviously intended to be a refrain, it adds strength to the idea that at one time, the two psalms were one.

Why are you in despair, O my soul?
And why are you disturbed within me?
Hope in God, for I shall again praise Him,
The help of my countenance,
and my God (v. 5).

PSALM 44

This is a lengthy psalm ascribed to the sons of Korah that deals with a review of a history of much of the nation. Every verse will not be dealt with here, but there will be an emphasis on the petition and the supplications made to God on behalf of the nation. The reader is encouraged to read the entire psalm at leisure.

Leupold[7] believes it is a psalm of David and places it in the history of David's struggle with the Syrians, the Edomites and the Ammonites recorded in 2 Samuel 8. He records, however, that Calvin insists that the writer is an unknown person who lived during the time of the Maccabees. All we know for certain is that it was a time when the army had been defeated, because it contains a strong lament that the Lord had allowed such a circumstance to come upon them.

> *O God, we have heard with our ears,*
> *Our fathers have told us,*
> *The work that Thou didst in their days,*
> *In the days of old.*
> *Thou with Thine own hand*
> *didst drive out the nations;*
> *Then Thou didst plant them;*
> *Thou didst afflict the peoples,*
> *Then Thou didst spread them abroad* (vv. 1, 2).

The implied question to God is, "Why are You not doing these same things for us now?"

> *Yet Thou hast rejected us*
> *and brought us to dishonor,*
> *And dost not go out with our armies.*
> *Thou dost cause us*
> *to turn back from the adversary;*
> *And those who hate us*
> *have taken spoil for themselves* (vv. 9, 10).

God is given as the effective cause for their defeat. In spite of my respect for Leupold, this does not sound much like the writing of David.

> *Thou dost give us*
> *as sheep to be eaten,*
> *And hast scattered us*
> *among the nations. . . .*
> *Thou dost make us*
> *a byword among the nations* (vv. 11, 14).

It's very difficult to see a postexilic date in the following:

All this has come upon us,
but we have not forgotten Thee,
And we have not dealt falsely
with Thy covenant (v. 17).

The writer could not have been in postexilic days because there was no doubt that Israel had been unfaithful to the covenant before God sent them into captivity. The only solid conclusion is that the historical setting is one not described in the Old Testament. This should not surprise us, because the Bible does not propose that the history of Israel is given in complete detail in the Old Testament. However, under the conditions described, we can understand the cry for help that closes the account.

Arouse Thyself, why dost Thou sleep, O Lord?
Awake, do not reject us forever (v. 23).

For our soul has sunk down into the dust;
Our body cleaves to the earth.
Rise up, be our help,
And redeem us for the sake
of Thy lovingkindness (vv. 25, 26).

Calvin may have been more on target than we may have expected.

Psalm 54

This psalm is David's cry when the Ziphites went to Saul and said, "Is not David hiding among us?" (1 Samuel 23:19, *NIV*; see also 26:1). These are the exact words found in the title of Psalm 54. Delitzsch[8] divides this short psalm into two parts. The first half prays for help and an answer:

Save me, O God, by Thy name,
And vindicate me by Thy power.
Hear my prayer, O God;
Give ear to the words of my mouth.
For strangers have risen against me,
And violent men have sought my life;
They have not set God before them.
Selah (vv. 1-3).

In the second part, the writer, assured of being heard, rejoices and makes a vow of thanksgiving:

Behold, God is my helper;
The Lord is the sustainer of my soul (v. 4).

Willingly I will sacrifice to Thee;
I will give thanks to Thy name,
O Lord, for it is good.
For He has delivered me
from all my trouble;
And my eye has looked with satisfaction
upon my enemies (vv. 6, 7).

PSALM 70

This psalm is an urgent cry for help. So far as we know, God never failed to hear David when he came to Him in earnest prayer. It is thought that this may indeed be a fragment of Psalm 40 because the verses are almost exact duplicates of the last five verses of that psalm (vv. 13–17). In both places, and in the same words, David speaks against his enemies.

O God, hasten to deliver me;
O Lord, hasten to my help!
Let those be ashamed and humiliated
Who seek my life;
Let those be turned back and dishonored
Who delight in my hurt.
Let those be turned back
because of their shame
Who say, "Aha, aha!" (vv. 1-3).

The latter part of the psalm speaks on behalf of God's mercies:

Let all who seek Thee
rejoice and be glad in Thee;
And let those who love Thy salvation
say continually, "Let God be magnified."
But I am afflicted and needy;
Hasten to me, O God!
Thou art my help and my deliverer;
O Lord, do not delay (vv. 4, 5).

Psalm 86

David begins this prayer by saying, "Incline Thine ear, O Lord, and answer me; for I am afflicted and needy" (v. 1).

This attitude could be called the trademark of David's attitude toward God and himself.

Do preserve my soul,
for I am a godly man;
O Thou my God,
save Thy servant

who trusts in Thee.
Be gracious to me, O Lord,
For to Thee I cry all day long.
Make glad the soul of Thy servant,
For to Thee, O Lord,
I lift up my soul (vv. 2-4).

We should not be surprised to find that God always came to David's aid. If our prayers were in the same spirit of humility and trust, we too would expect God to answer.

In the day of my trouble
I shall call upon Thee,
For Thou wilt answer me (v. 7).

For Thou art great
and doest wondrous deeds;
Thou alone art God (v. 10).

Then David's petition turns to his spiritual growth:

Teach me Thy way, O Lord;
I will walk in Thy truth;
Unite my heart
to fear Thy name (v. 11).

In the closing verses he implores God to turn to him and impart strength with a sign for his deliverance:

Turn to me, and be gracious to me;
Oh grant Thy strength to Thy servant,
And save the son of Thy handmaid.
Show me a sign for good,
That those who hate me may see it,

and be ashamed,
Because Thou, O Lord,
hast helped me
and comforted me (vv. 16, 17).

Psalm 88

This psalm is without doubt the saddest and most pitiful of all the psalms. From the beginning to the end, there seems to be no break in the sad recounting of trials. Some reckon it to be the prayer of a shut-in who suffered from a prolonged and incurable disease. In fact, some have concluded the writer was a leper, as may be implied in verse 8. But the truth is, we know little about the time of writing or the person who wrote it. All we really know is that it is a psalm for the suffering.

Ellicott[9] gives the title as "A song or psalm for the sons of Korah, to the chief Musician upon Mahalath Leannoth, Maschil of Heman the Ezrahite." He further explains that the term *Mahalath* is also found in Psalm 53 and seems to refer to sickness or distress. It may well be the name of a tune of a melancholy nature. The term *Maschil* is sometimes used with didactic psalms and could refer to understanding. Using these two terms together may indicate that it is a song to help others to understand those who are suffering. In the title, Heman the Ezrahite is the Heman of 1 Chronicles 2:6 and 1 Kings 4:31. We know from these scriptures that he was one of the sons of Zerah and that Solomon was said to be wiser than he. This would indicate a strong recognition for his wisdom and understanding. The title seems to be three combined into one, but with some help, it can be unraveled.

O Lord, the God of my salvation,
I have cried out by day
and in the night before Thee.
Let my prayer come before Thee;
Incline Thine ear to my cry!
For my soul has had enough troubles,
And my life has drawn near to Sheol.
I am reckoned among those
who go down to the pit;
I have become like a man without strength,
Forsaken among the dead,
Like the slain who lie in the grave,
Whom Thou dost remember no more,
And they are cut off from Thy hand (vv. 1-5).

Here we not only hear the lament of a seriously ill person, but we also hear one who has no hope beyond the grave. Except in verse 1, where the psalmist acknowledges that it is the Lord who saves him, there seems to be no point in his lament.

Thou hast put me in the lowest pit,
In dark places, in the depths.
Thy wrath has rested upon me,
And Thou hast afflicted me
with all Thy waves. Selah.
Thou hast removed my acquaintances
far from me;
Thou hast made me
an object of loathing to them;
I am shut up and cannot go out (vv. 6-8).

The writer seems to be saying that God is to blame for all of his sorrow. The *Thou* and *Thy* refer directly to the act of God so far as the writer is concerned. If he would only express some hope in his grief, we could feel so much better.

My eye has wasted away
because of affliction;
I have called upon Thee every day, O Lord;
I have spread out my hands to Thee.
Wilt Thou perform wonders for the dead?
Will the departed spirits
rise and praise Thee? Selah (vv. 9, 10).

In spite of his lack of hope, he does not cease to call. Is that the faith for which we look?

But I, O Lord,
have cried out to Thee for help,
And in the morning
my prayer comes before Thee.
O Lord, why dost Thou reject my soul?
Why dost Thou hide Thy
face from me? (vv. 13, 14).

He cannot get past the idea that his affliction is a sign of God's rejection.

I was afflicted and
about to die from my youth on;
I suffer Thy terrors;
I am overcome.
Thy burning anger
has passed over me;
Thy terrors have destroyed me.

They have surrounded me
like water all day long;
They have encompassed me altogether.
Thou hast removed lover and friend
far from me;
My acquaintances are in darkness (vv. 15-18).

So ends the most distressing psalm of the entire book. I would like to go to him and explain, but the time is past. How my heart mourns for one who sees darkness as his closest friend. This lack of faith is one reason why we think that the author was not the Ezrahite of 1 Chronicles 15:17, who was one of David's music leaders. He wrote the beautiful Psalm 89, which is full of hope and confidence. This psalm will be addressed in another section.

This hopelessness could be a national picture rather than a personal one. There was a time when the prophets pictured God as abandoning Israel. Such is a possible interpretation for the psalm.

Psalm 140

David had many enemies. This psalm describes how they drove him closer to God. The more he was criticized, the closer he came to God for protection. This is a pattern we would do well to imitate today. Some offer alternatives to the authorship but, in the absence of significant reason otherwise, I am inclined to stay with the Davidic authorship suggested by Rabbinic tradition. This psalm, like the next one, is a strong supplication for deliverance, not only from the enemies in his kingdom, but also from the evil and treacherous men without.

Rescue me, O Lord,
from evil men;
Preserve me from violent men,
Who devise evil things
in their hearts;
They continually stir up wars.
They sharpen their tongues
as a serpent;
Poison of a viper
is under their lips. Selah (vv. 1-3).

David was both a man of war and a man of peace. He went to God to maintain peace, but he prepared for war and was an unbeatable foe when that was the only option.

Keep me, O Lord,
from the hands of the wicked;
Preserve me from violent men,
Who have purposed
to trip up my feet.
The proud have hidden
a trap for me, and cords;
They have spread a net
by the wayside;
They have set
snares for me. Selah (vv. 4, 5).

But David, a strong man of war, looks to God for deliverance.

I said to the Lord,
"Thou art my God;
Give ear, O Lord,

to the voice of my supplications.
"O God the Lord,
the strength of my salvation,
Thou hast covered my head
in the day of battle.
"Do not grant, O Lord,
the desires of the wicked;
Do not promote his evil device,
lest they be exalted. Selah" (vv. 6-8).

In his supplication, David argues first that God is his help; secondly, that if the proud won over him, they would become even more wicked.

"As for the head of
those who surround me,
May the mischief of
their lips cover them.
"May burning coals
fall upon them;
May they be cast
into the fire,
Into deep pits from which
they cannot rise.
"May a slanderer not
be established in the earth;
May evil hunt
the violent man speedily" (vv. 9-11).

Here we have another imprecatory element, where David prays for the destruction of his enemies. But we may consider that God's intention was to destroy evil and wicked men, so the prayer is a request for God to do just that.

I know that the Lord will maintain
the cause of the afflicted,
And justice for the poor.
Surely the righteous
will give thanks to Thy name;
The upright will dwell
in Thy presence (vv. 12, 13).

David makes it plain that he does not pray against the upright, but he prays that the evil shall perish. According to Psalm 1, that is exactly God's plan.

PSALM 141

This psalm, like the one preceding and following it, is a supplication of David that the righteous may be blessed and the evil men punished.

O Lord, I call upon Thee;
hasten to me!
Give ear to my voice
when I call to Thee!
May my prayer be counted
as incense before Thee;
The lifting up of my hands
as the evening offering (vv. 1, 2).

Because of this portion, this psalm has been regarded as an evening prayer. We do not know that it was so intended, but it certainly lends itself to that interpretation.

Set a guard, O Lord,
over my mouth;
Keep watch over

the door of my lips.
Do not incline my heart
to any evil thing,
To practice deeds of wickedness
With men who do iniquity;
And do not let me eat
of their delicacies (vv. 3, 4).

This supplication is for personal holiness. David does not want to be a partaker of that which he condemns, so he cries to God for the power to not walk in wicked ways.

Let the righteous
smite me in kindness
and reprove me;
It is oil upon the head;
Do not let my head refuse it,
For still my prayer is against
their wicked deeds.
Their judges are thrown down
by the sides of the rock,
And they hear my words,
for they are pleasant.
As when one plows
and breaks open the earth,
Our bones have been scattered
at the mouth of Sheol (vv. 5-7).

The child of God should not fear the rebuke of the righteous man because this is the voice of God calling him away from evil. But the evil has no right to rebuke the righteous.

For my eyes are toward Thee,
O God, the Lord;

In Thee I take refuge;
do not leave me defenseless.
Keep me from the jaws of the trap
which they have set for me,
And from the snares
of those who do iniquity.
Let the wicked fall
into their own nets,
While I pass by safely (vv. 8-10).

Sometimes the righteous hold their peace when they are oppressed. They should cry out to God who has promised to be their security. This is the positive side of prayer—God will save the righteous while He casts out the wicked.

8

Historical Psalms

The Book of Psalms is not primarily a book of history. It does, however, provide songs and poems dealing with historical events. These events cover the entire Old Testament from the time of Israel in Egypt, through the reigns of David and Solomon, the fall of the northern kingdom to the Assyrians, the destruction of the Temple and the land of Judah, the Babylonian Captivity and return. Also, this history includes the building of the second Temple with songs composed for use in the second Temple as a part of post-Captivity worship.

The study of this section will require a little more concentration than normal because the events will not be in chronological order. We will follow rather the sequence of Psalm numbers, the first of which (Psalm 74) has its setting during the Babylonian Captivity (605-538 B.C.). It will help to remember that Judah fell in three stages—605 B.C., 597 B.C. and 586 B.C.

The following psalm (Psalm 76) has its historical setting

prior to the fall of the northern kingdom in 722 B.C. For this reason, the reader will of necessity need to understand some order of the sequence of the history of the Old Testament.

The question could be asked why I have not arranged them in chronological order to help the reader follow more easily. This was considered, but the fact that some historical psalms attempt to cover the entire span of God's dealing with Israel makes it impractical. However, I have attempted to explain and date some of the more specific settings. The dates used will be approximate because some historians do not agree on exact dates, and some events do not always mention kings or other means by which a date may be determined. Each date used as an aid will be preceded by c., indicating that it represents a time which is a close approximation. This procedure will be followed in chapters 8 and 9 as they cover the majority of Old Testament history.

The purpose of the Historical Psalms was not to teach Hebrew history, for it was written to people who knew it well. However, for us who live 2,000-3,000 years later, we need to have a setting which will give the material the meaning the psalmist intended.

Psalm 74

There can be no doubt about the historical setting of this song of lament by Asaph. It was written after the destruction of Jerusalem and the Temple (c. 586 B.C.). The verses themselves reveal the condition of the national disaster.

> *O God, why hast Thou rejected us forever?*
> *Why does Thine anger smoke*
> *against the sheep of Thy pasture?* (v. 1).

With the destruction of the Temple, it seemed that Israel had no future.

Remember Thy congregation,
which Thou hast purchased of old,
Which Thou hast redeemed to be
the tribe of Thine inheritance;
And Mount Zion,
where Thou hast dwelt (v. 2).

Notice the past tense *dwelt* indicated what God had done. This leaves no doubt that the psalm was written in the period of the Exile.

Thine adversaries have roared
in the midst of Thy meeting place;
They have set up their own standards
for signs (v. 4).

And now all its carved work
They smash with hatchet and hammers.
They have burned Thy sanctuary
to the ground;
They have defiled the dwelling place
of Thy name (vv. 6, 7).

But in the face of all this, the psalmist dares to ask for hope and deliverance.

Do not deliver the soul of Thy turtledove
to the wild beast;
Do not forget the life
of Thine afflicted forever (v. 19).

Let not the oppressed return dishonored;

Let the afflicted and needy
praise Thy name.
Do arise, O God,
and plead Thine own cause;
Remember how the foolish man
reproaches Thee all day long (vv. 21, 22).

Psalm 76

The historical setting of this psalm describes the deliverance of Judah and Jerusalem from the armies of Sennacherib, the king of Assyria, who took captive the northern kingdom of Israel (c. 722 B.C.). Judah and Jerusalem were threatened at that time, but God delivered them out of the hands of Assyria. It was about 100 years later that God permitted Judah and Jerusalem to fall to the Babylonians (c. 605-586 B.C.). It was around this later event that Psalm 74 was composed.

Psalm 76 (of Asaph) is opened with a praise to God for delivering Jerusalem:

God is known in Judah;
His name is great in Israel.
And His tabernacle is in Salem;
His dwelling place also is in Zion.
There He broke the flaming arrows,
The shield, and the sword,
and the weapons of war. Selah (vv. 1-3).

The nation of Judah realized that man's hand had not delivered them from the enemy, but God himself had intervened.

Thou didst cause judgment
to be heard from heaven;
The earth feared, and was still,
When God arose to judgment (vv. 8, 9).

In fact, the prophet Isaiah had promised that the Lord would destroy the armies of Sennacherib, king of Assyria, when the men of Hezekiah came to him for help (c. 701 B.C.).

"The Virgin Daughter of Zion
despises you and mocks you.
The Daughter of Jerusalem
tosses her head as you flee"
(2 Kings 19:21, *NIV*).

The psalmist closes his document with the following warning to the kings who would attack Judah:

He will cut off the spirit of princes;
He is feared by the kings of the earth (v. 12).

Psalm 77

This is another song of Asaph, a celebrated singer in the temple of David. There may well have been a descendant of the same name who lived and served later, but there is little certainty about the date of the writing. The internal evidence describes a time of great trouble. The writer goes through a time of genuine doubt as to God's purpose. Later he comes through with a confidence that is at least partially restored.

Jeduthun is mentioned in the psalm title, but this does not mean that he is the author. The phrase "according to Jeduthun" probably means that it was to be sung the way Jeduthun determined.

When I remember God, then I am disturbed;
When I sigh, then my spirit grows faint. Selah.
Thou hast held my eyelids open;
I am so troubled that I cannot speak (vv. 3, 4).

The writer was able to draw no strength from God because he did not believe God was hearing him.

I have considered the days of old,
The years of long ago.
I will remember my song in the night;
I will meditate with my heart;
And my spirit ponders (vv. 5, 6).

The writer had seen better days, when he had sung and rejoiced, but these were days of long ago. This causes many scholars to set a captivity date for the psalm (post 605 B.C.), but we will see later that this is not borne out.

Has His lovingkindness ceased forever?
Has His promise come to an end forever?
Has God forgotten to be gracious?
Or has He in anger
withdrawn His compassion? Selah (vv. 8, 9).

Each of these questions raise doubt about the nature of God. Had God changed? Could the love the psalmist thought was unlimited actually be a limited love? Could God make a promise and then fail to keep it? Seldom do we read a psalm that expresses such deep doubt about the nature of God. But the psalmist remembers God's help in the past and begins to find his balance.

I shall remember the deeds of the Lord;
Surely I will remember Thy wonders of old.

I will meditate on all Thy work,
And muse on Thy deeds (vv. 11, 12).

The following portion of the psalm tells two of the mighty things that God had done for Israel:

- He brought them out of Egypt (v. 15) (c. 1445 B.C.).
- He opened the Red Sea (v. 19).

If this was written during the Captivity, he could have listed many other miracles. As it stands, the fact that the writer did not go beyond Moses for his material seems to place the psalm at an early date with the circumstance unknown. But he who remembers God's goodness to man is on his way back to faith.

Psalm 78

This is the longest psalm of its kind in the book. It is, in fact, the only one intended to concentrate on the national failings. Its purpose is to establish Judah and reject Ephraim because of disloyalty and idolatry. It also emphasizes the rejection of the northern tribe of Israel (which was often called *Ephraim*) in order to represent the northern tribes as a unit.

The date of writing is uncertain, but according to Ellicott the mention of "high places" (v. 58) suggests it was written during the time of Hezekiah[1] (c. 520 B.C.). The psalm is sometimes referred to as *epi-didactic*, which means it would teach through telling a story. Because of its length, we will use selected portions to tell the story of Israel's history through its failures.

For He established a testimony in Jacob,
And appointed a law in Israel,
Which He commanded our fathers,

That they should teach them
to their children (v. 5).

This tells us that the author intends to tell the history through Israel's defeats, rather than her victories. The writer begins by declaring the revelation of God's law at Sinai.

And not be like their fathers,
A stubborn and rebellious generation,
A generation that did not prepare its heart,
And whose spirit
was not faithful to God (v. 8).

Note the unusual accusations of the people of Israel by the author. This is what set this historical account apart from the others in the Book of Psalms.

The sons of Ephraim were archers
equipped with bows,
Yet they turned back in the day of battle.
They did not keep the covenant of God,
And refused to walk in His law (vv. 9, 10).

The tribe of Ephraim is singled out for its failure to trust God. The purpose in this was to demonstrate that they could not be God's chosen people. The following scriptures are cited as a review of the history of what God had done for His people:

- God divided the sea for them (v. 13) (c. 1445 B.C.).
- God went before them by a cloud to cover them by day and with fire to guide them and light their path by night (v. 14).
- He divided the rock in the desert and brought forth a stream that followed them (v. 15).

- He supplied manna for the people to eat (v. 24).
- God "rained meat down on them like dust, flying birds like sand on the seashore" (v. 27, *NIV*).
- He displayed His miraculous signs in Egypt (v. 43).
- He turned rivers into blood (v. 44).
- He struck down all the firstborn of Egypt (v. 51).
- He drove out the nations before them (v. 55).
- He settled the tribes of Israel in the land of Canaan (v. 55) (c. 1400).

But note how the people responded to God's goodness:

- They rebelled against the Most High (v. 56) (Sinai and following c. 1446).
- They were disloyal and faithless (v. 57).
- They provoked Him with their high places (v. 58).
- They aroused His jealousy with their idols (v. 58).

These verses would apply to the period beginning with Solomon. We then see how God responded to the faithlessness of the people:

- God rejected Israel completely (v. 59).
- He abandoned the Tabernacle at Shiloh (v. 60).
- "He sent the ark of his might into captivity" (v. 61, *NIV*).
- He delivered His people to the sword (v. 62).
- Fire consumed their young men (v. 63).
- Their priests fell by the sword (v. 64) (Saul c. 1030).

Verse 61 occurred at the death of Eli and the rise of Samuel as judge. The last few verses we need to look at were written to show the mercies of God after His people rejected Him:

> *Then the Lord awoke as if from sleep,*
> *Like a warrior overcome by wine.*

And He drove His adversaries backward;
He put on them an everlasting reproach.
He also rejected the tent of Joseph,
And did not choose the tribe of Ephraim,
But chose the tribe of Judah,
[David establishes Jerusalem c. 970 B.C.]
Mount Zion which He loved.
And He built His sanctuary like the heights,
Like the earth which He has founded forever.
He also chose David His servant,
And took him from the sheepfolds;
From the care of the ewes
with suckling lambs He brought him,
To shepherd Jacob, His people,
And Israel His inheritance.
So he shepherded them according
to the integrity of his heart,
And guided them
with his skillful hands (vv. 65–72).

David's establishment of Jerusalem would begin with the capture of the city and the bringing of the ark of God to make it the center of worship.

Psalm 79

Leupold[2] says that this psalm of Asaph is both a lament over the destruction of Jerusalem (vv. 1-4) and a prayer for help (vv. 5-13). He breaks them into four subdivisions.

O God, the nations have invaded
Thine inheritance;
They have defiled Thy holy temple;

They have laid Jerusalem in ruins.
They have given the dead bodies
of Thy servants
for food to the birds of the heavens,
The flesh of Thy godly ones
to the beasts of the earth (vv. 1, 2).

In verse 1 the Temple is said to be "defiled" instead of destroyed. However, the next verse pictures Jerusalem in rubble, which causes most scholars to place this event as a part of the Babylonian destruction and captivity. No other incident in the Old Testament would fit that picture.

They have poured out their blood like water
round about Jerusalem;
And there was no one to bury them (v. 3).

The attackers did not bother to bury the dead, and the captives were not allowed to do so. They were herded into a forced march out of the city toward Babylon.

We have become a reproach to our neighbors,
A scoffing and derision
to those around us (v. 4).

History tells of the Edomites who gathered to watch the destruction of Jerusalem and rejoiced that Israel was being punished. The words above are also recorded in Psalm 44:13.

How long, O Lord?
Wilt Thou be angry forever?
Will Thy jealousy burn like fire?
Pour out Thy wrath upon the nations

which do not know Thee,
And upon the kingdoms
which do not call upon Thy name;
For they have devoured Jacob,
And laid waste his habitation.
Do not remember the iniquities
of our forefathers against us;
Let Thy compassion come quickly to meet us;
For we are brought very low (vv. 5-8).

Two primary questions puzzled the psalmist: (1) Was the God they had served capable of remaining angry forever? The sin mentioned here is the sin of their forefathers, and it does not seem to be reasonable that God would hold them responsible. (2) Why did God not destroy the evil people instead of the good people who had worshiped at the Temple? What benefit was there in serving a God who would destroy the righteous and let the sinner go unpunished? Why would He allow the people who destroyed the Temple and killed the people go unpunished?

Help us, O God of our salvation,
for the glory of Thy name;
And deliver us, and forgive our sins,
for Thy name's sake.
Why should the nations say,
"Where is their God?"
Let there be known
among the nations in our sight,
Vengeance for the blood of Thy servants,
which has been shed.
Let the groaning of the prisoner
come before Thee;

According to the greatness of Thy power
preserve those who are doomed to die
(vv. 9-11).

The writer of the psalm acknowledges that this was God's doing. It was not just because one nation was stronger than the other; it was because God willed it to happen. He realizes that it was not only the fathers who had sinned, but the whole nation had also done evil. They were guilty, and in verse 9 the author pleads to God for forgiveness. He does, however, feel justified in asking God to punish the guilty. Who among the heathen would want to worship a God who allowed His people to be destroyed in such a manner? Many had been killed by the sword, and many more would die along the way. Furthermore, those who survived would be held captive and face an awful fate. Surely a just God would hear their prayers.

And return to our neighbors
sevenfold into their bosom
The reproach with which
they have reproached Thee, O Lord.
So we Thy people
and the sheep of Thy pasture
Will give thanks to Thee forever;
To all generations
we will tell of Thy praise (vv. 12, 13).

The term *sevenfold* mentioned in verse 12 does not, in all likelihood, refer to a simple seven times the measurement of punishment. Rather, it would refer to the number *seven*, which throughout Scripture is used as the number of perfection or completeness.

The psalm closes with a sacred vow that God would be praised forever when He had indeed brought deliverance, as He surely would. The Hallelujah Psalms, which close the Book of Psalms, give evidence of the fulfillment of this vow.

Psalm 80

Leupold[3] calls this psalm "The Anguished Cry of a Desolate Nation." The subject matter seems to be the same as the preceding one. Certainly the scene is one of national disaster.

> *Oh, give ear, Shepherd of Israel,*
> *Thou who dost lead Joseph like a flock;*
> *Thou who art enthroned above the cherubim,*
> *shine forth!*
> *Before Ephraim and Benjamin and Manasseh,*
> *stir up Thy power,*
> *And come to save us!* (vv. 1, 2).

It cannot be disputed that this is a plea for God's help when Israel was held powerless by a foreign nation. The fact that verse 2 mentions the northern tribes of Ephraim and Manasseh would argue that it was not the Babylonian Captivity, although some scholars believe that this does not prove conclusively that it was not. Also verse 9 seems to imply that both the northern and southern empires still existed. Verse 1 certainly implies this. But it is past tense, so it is not conclusive.

Ellicott[4] suggests that it was at the time when Assyria and Egypt made the whole country a battleground, but he is not inclined to rule out other possibilities. If this is accurate, the time element would describe conditions just prior to 721 B.C.

O God, restore us,
And cause Thy face to shine upon us,
and we will be saved.
O Lord God of hosts,
How long wilt Thou be angry
with the prayer of Thy people?
Thou hast fed them
with the bread of tears,
And Thou hast made them
to drink tears in large measure.
Thou dost make us
an object of contention to our neighbors;
And our enemies laugh among themselves.
O God of hosts, restore us,
And cause Thy face to shine upon us,
and we will be saved (vv. 3-7).

The prayer for restoration represents a genuine faith, in that verses 3 and 7 both include the prayer that "we will be saved." The hope of restoration, in such a time as Israel faced, was the beginning of the restoration itself. God always responds to hope born out of trust in His mercy.

Thou didst remove a vine from Egypt;
Thou didst drive out the nations,
and didst plant it.
Thou didst clear the ground before it,
And it took deep root
and filled the land (vv. 8, 9).

The vine is obviously Israel, and the nations are the people of Canaan who were driven out so that the ground could be prepared for God's people. This takes our history back to the Exodus of Israel from Egypt.

The mountains were covered with its shadow;
And the cedars of God with its boughs.
It was sending out its branches to the sea,
And its shoots to the River (vv. 10, 11).

The extent of Israel's growth is described by the growth of the vine. The sea referred to was the Mediterranean, and the river was the Euphrates. Israel's expansion was during the last half of David's reign and the first half of Solomon's reign. This period is known as the "Golden Age" of Israel.

Why hast Thou broken down its hedges,
So that all who pass that way pick its fruit?
A boar from the forest eats it away,
And whatever moves in the field feeds on it.
O God of hosts, turn again now,
we beseech Thee;
Look down from heaven and see,
and take care of this vine,
Even the shoot which
Thy right hand has planted,
And on the son whom Thou
hast strengthened for Thyself (vv. 12-15).

A city without walls was no city because it would be open to the ravages of both man and beasts. Its inhabitants would have no protection. The Assyrians overran northern Israel c. 722 B.C. This picture could be shortly before.

It is burned with fire,
it is cut down;
They perish at the rebuke
of Thy countenance.

Let Thy hand be upon
the man of Thy right hand,
Upon the son of man
whom Thou didst make
strong for Thyself.
Then we shall not
turn back from Thee;
Revive us, and we
will call upon Thy name (vv. 16-18).

God must restore His vine if it is to bear fruit. The man at His right hand was the king upon his throne, who moved as God gave the command. Was this nation Israel? If so, the time element would offer proof that she had not yet fallen to Assyria. Some think the reference to the "son of man" was a direct reference to the Messiah. But in this case, it seems to underscore the fact that Israel was a son in the sense that the heathen nations were not.

O Lord God of hosts, restore us;
Cause Thy face to shine upon us,
and we will be saved (v. 19).

This last verse is evidence that Israel believed that salvation was possible only through the Lord God of hosts, who ruled over all the earth. It could not be by their might and power because they were no match for the nations coming against them. Salvation and deliverance, in the writer's mind, was possible only if God turned and delivered them.

Psalm 81

The title is "For the choir director; on the Gittith," which suggests, as in other places, the instrument from Gath on which the music was played. The song itself was obviously meant for a national observance, but just which one is difficult to tell. Ellicott[5] suggests the Feast of Tabernacles, but he agrees it could be used at others. Clarke[6] believes that it may have been used for the Feast of Trumpets (on the first day of Tishri), or the Feast of Tabernacles (on the 15th day of the same month). Jewish tradition seems to lend support to one of these, since the Jewish Targums insert the name Tishri into verse 3 (Leupold[7]). Some scholars place the first three verses as a kind of introduction to the rest of the psalm.

Sing for joy to God our strength;
Shout joyfully to the God of Jacob.
Raise a song, strike the timbrel,
The sweet sounding lyre with the harp.
Blow the trumpet at the new moon,
At the full moon, on our feast day (vv. 1-3).

The first verse seems to call for a religious festival, but it names none in particular. The second verse is probably directed to the Levites, who supplied the music for such a festival. It specifies a psalm and designates the timbrel, the harp and the lyre specifically. Verse 3 was probably addressed to the priests whose duty it was to blow the horn for sacred gatherings. The trumpet (ram's horn) was blown at the festival of the full moon when both the Passover and the Feast of Tabernacles were celebrated.

For it is a statute for Israel,
An ordinance of the God of Jacob.
He established it for a testimony in Joseph,
When he went throughout the land of Egypt.
I heard a language that I did not know:

"I relieved his shoulder of the burden,
His hands were freed from the basket.
"You called in trouble, and I rescued you;
I answered you in the hiding place of thunder;
I proved you at the waters of Meribah."
Selah (vv. 4-7).

This observance was a decree for the children of Israel because they were set free from the burdens of Egypt. The testing at Meribah is an incident from Exodus 17, when Moses struck the rock and God sent forth water for the children of Israel.

"Hear, O My people, and I will admonish you;
O Israel, if you would listen to Me!
Let there be no strange god among you;
Nor shall you worship any foreign god.
"I, the Lord, am your God,
Who brought you up from the land of Egypt;
Open your mouth wide and I will fill it.
"But My people did not listen to My voice;
And Israel did not obey Me.
"So I gave them over
to the stubbornness of their heart,
To walk in their own devices" (vv. 8-12).

The reminder to have no strange gods is a repetition of the first commandment, which Israel had often broken. His promise is that if they would obey the command, He would see that their needs would be supplied. But Israel rejected the command of their God, and He gave them over to their own devices to follow their own stubborn ways. The historical time would have been shortly after the Exodus.

"Oh that My people would listen to Me,
That Israel would walk in My ways!
"I would quickly subdue their enemies,
And turn My hand against their adversaries.
"Those who hate the Lord
would pretend obedience to Him;
And their time of punishment
would be forever.
"But I would feed you
with the finest of the wheat;
And with honey from the rock
I would satisfy you" (vv. 13-16).

God promises His people that if they would walk in His ways, He would quickly subdue their enemies and fight their battles for them. Verse 15 declares this to be an everlasting covenant. An obedient people would be fed with the finest wheat and with an abundance of honey.

PSALM 82

The theme of this psalm of Asaph is the necessity of having wise judges in the nation of Israel. According to the Talmud (Delitzsch[8]) it is the *Tuesday Psalm* in which God speaks as a prophet and pronounces divine judgment. Jesus called attention to this psalm in John 10:34-36, when He explained that He did not blaspheme when He said He was God's Son. His argument was that God's people were called His sons.

God takes His stand in His own congregation;
He judges in the midst of the rulers.
How long will you judge unjustly,

And show partiality to the wicked?
Selah (Psalm 82:1, 2).

In verse 1, the term *rulers* is also translated *elohim* in some versions (*NIV,* "gods"). Here the term *elohim,* which is the name for God in Genesis 1, is used to describe the judges of Israel. Note that the translation uses *elohim,* not *Elohim,* suggesting that the judges were minor gods. He then accuses them of showing partiality, which increases wickedness in the land.

Vindicate the weak and fatherless;
Do justice to the afflicted and destitute.
Rescue the weak and needy;
Deliver them out of
the hand of the wicked (vv. 3, 4).

The purpose of godly judges in the land was to defend the weak, the poor, and the oppressed and to deliver them from the hand of the wicked. He reminded them that justice was the fundamental virtue of society.

They do not know nor do they understand;
They walk about in darkness;
All the foundations of the earth
are shaken (v. 5).

Leupold[9] calls this verse a divine soliloquy. The judges give unjust judgment, and God will call them into judgment to give account for this. A judge cannot overlook the command of God and go unpunished. This would cause the foundations of the earth to be destroyed. David used this concept in Psalm 11 when he asked what one was to do if the foundations were destroyed.

I said, "You are gods,
And all of you are sons of the Most High.
"Nevertheless you will die like men,
And fall like any one of the princes."
Arise, O God, judge the earth!
For it is Thou who dost possess
all the nations (82:6-8).

Again, the psalmist refers to the judges as "gods" (or "elohim") and "sons of the Most High." But verse 7 says that since they act as men, they will die as men. In the final verse, the psalmist declares that the judgment in the earth will be right only if God comes forth to judge the earth. Some see in this a plea for God's return to judge the earth as Christians today believe He will do.

Psalm 101

This psalm of David has as its theme the qualities of a good ruler. Some have thought it might have first been sung when David first ascended to the throne. It is a model by which a king should govern.

I will sing of lovingkindness and justice,
To Thee, O Lord, I will sing praises.
I will give heed to the blameless way.
When wilt Thou come to me?
I will walk within my house
in the integrity of my heart (vv. 1, 2).

The first verse underscores the fact that it is not enough to sing, but singing unto the Lord is a highly recommended form of worship. The question of verse 2, "When wilt Thou come to me?" may have reference to the ark of the covenant, which represented the presence of the Lord. If so, this would have been when the ark remained in the house of Obed-Edom, where David had left it when Uzzah was killed as the ark was being transported to Jerusalem. At that time David asked the question, "How can the ark of the Lord come to me?" (2 Samuel 6:9) (c. 970 B.C.). In the context of Psalm 101:2, he seems to be saying that he intends to conduct himself in such a way that the Lord (represented by the ark) would be willing to dwell with him. That would mean he desired to walk upright before his people and in his private life.

I will set no worthless thing before my eyes;
I hate the work of those who fall away;
It shall not fasten its grip on me.
A perverse heart shall depart from me;
I will know no evil (vv. 3, 4).

Verses 3 and 4 indicate that David's intent was to put away evil—both internal and external—so God would be pleased with him. He is determined to have nothing to do with any wicked thing as he walked before the people.

Whoever secretly slanders his neighbor,
him I will destroy;
No one who has a haughty look
and an arrogant heart will I endure.
My eyes shall be upon the faithful of the land,
that they may dwell with me;
He who walks in a blameless way
is the one who will minister to me.
He who practices deceit
shall not dwell within my house;

He who speaks falsehood
shall not maintain his position
before me (vv. 5-7).

David is determined to have no one in his presence who slanders others or exhibits a proud heart. He will seek out the faithful to hold offices in his kingdom. Deceit and falsehood will not be tolerated in anyone answerable to him on the throne. He is determined to have a perfect rule. Perhaps this is the foreshadowing of One who would be raised up from the line of David who would indeed accomplish what David wanted to do.

PSALM 105

This psalm is not titled. According to Clarke[10], it seems to be associated with the preceding psalm. However, since that carries no authorship or time, we have little to suggest authorship. Halley[11] calls it and the one following, "Two Historical Psalms," which give a poetic summary of Israel's history with highest praise being given to God for His deliverance and care of Israel.

We do know that some of the song belongs to David. In 1 Chronicles 16:7 we find that David committed to Asaph a psalm of thanksgiving and that verses 8 through 12 are identical to the first five verses of this psalm.

Oh give thanks to the Lord,
call upon His name;
Make known His deeds among the peoples.
Sing to Him, sing praises to Him;
Speak of all His wonders.
Glory in His holy name;

Let the heart of those
who seek the Lord be glad.
Seek the Lord and His strength;
Seek His face continually.
Remember His wonders which He has done,
His marvels, and the judgments
uttered by His mouth (vv. 1-5).

We know then, that the first portion was written by David. Someone could have used these first five verses as an introduction to a psalm they wanted to write concerning the many miracles that had taken place in the history of Israel. Since a number of psalms have been attributed to Asaph, who was the music director for David, it is reasonable that he could have produced another psalm with these verses as an introduction. In that case, the reason for his name not to be attached remains mute.

Because the evidence from 1 Chronicles tells us that David's song celebrated the occasion of the ark being brought to the city of Jerusalem, it is possible that this psalm was also written to commemorate that event. At any rate, the writer goes back to Abraham to begin his historical sketch (c. 2000 B.C.).

O seed of Abraham, His servant,
O sons of Jacob, His chosen ones!
He is the Lord our God;
His judgments are in all the earth.
He has remembered His covenant forever,
The word which He commanded
to a thousand generations,
The covenant which He made with Abraham,

And His oath to Isaac.
Then He confirmed it to Jacob for a statute,
To Israel as an everlasting covenant,
Saying, "To you I will give the land of Canaan
As the portion of your inheritance,"
When they were only a few men in number,
Very few, and strangers in it.
And they wandered about
from nation to nation,
From one kingdom to another people.
He permitted no man to oppress them,
And He reproved kings for their sakes:
"Do not touch My anointed ones,
And do My prophets no harm" (vv. 6-15).

God made a covenant with Abraham and renewed it with Isaac and Jacob, that He would give to Abraham and his seed the land of Canaan. Verse 11 tells us that this is an everlasting covenant. For their sakes, He rebuked kings and protected His prophets from harm. This covenant will one day be renewed in the time of the Messiah.

And He called for a famine upon the land;
He broke the whole staff of bread.
He sent a man before them,
Joseph, who was sold as a slave.
They afflicted his feet with fetters,
He himself was laid in irons;
Until the time that his word came to pass,
The word of the Lord tested him.
The king sent and released him,
The ruler of peoples, and set him free.

He made him lord of his house,
And ruler over all his possessions,
To imprison his princes at will,
That he might teach his elders wisdom
(vv. 16-22).

The story of Joseph is recounted to emphasize that God sent him into Egypt, allowed him to be placed in shackles, and then brought him out and made him a ruler in the land under Pharaoh.

Israel also came into Egypt;
Thus Jacob sojourned in the land of Ham.
And He caused His people to be very fruitful,
And made them stronger
than their adversaries.
He turned their heart to hate His people,
To deal craftily with his servants.
He sent Moses His servant,
And Aaron whom He had chosen.
They performed His wondrous acts
among them,
And miracles in the land of Ham (vv. 23-27).

Then God sent Israel into Egypt, where they grew to great numbers. Because they feared them, the Egyptians placed them in slavery. God sent Moses to deliver the Israelites after they cried out to Him for deliverance. Their march out of the land of Ham was a part of God's promise in the days of Noah. Egypt was the land settled by Ham after the Flood.

He sent darkness and made it dark;
And they did not rebel against His words.

He turned their waters into blood,
And caused their fish to die.
Their land swarmed with frogs
Even in the chambers of their kings.
He spoke, and there came a swarm of flies
And gnats in all their territory.
He gave them hail for rain,
And flaming fire in their land.
He struck down their vines also
and their fig trees,
And shattered the trees of their territory.
He spoke, and locusts came,
And young locusts, even without number,
And ate up all vegetation in their land,
And ate up the fruit of their ground.
He also struck down
all the first-born in their land,
The first fruits of all their vigor (vv. 28-36).

The writer recounts the plagues that fell upon Egypt to demonstrate the length to which God would go to deliver His people, including the killing of the firstborn of Egypt. This is the history of Israel based on the goodness of God to them.

Then He brought them out
with silver and gold;
And among His tribes
there was not one who stumbled.
Egypt was glad when they departed;
For the dread of them
had fallen upon them.
He spread a cloud for a covering,

And fire to illumine by night.
They asked, and He brought quail,
And satisfied them with the bread of heaven.
He opened the rock, and water flowed out;
It ran in the dry places like a river (vv. 37-41).

The Israelites came out of Egypt laden with much silver and gold. The people were happy to see them leave and gave gifts to persuade them to go. God also sent a cloud to cover them by day and fire to guide them by night. He provided food in the form of manna and quail, and He supplied water from the rock, which formed a stream that followed them. In short, God gave them all that they needed.

For He remembered His holy word
With Abraham, His servant;
And He brought forth His people with joy,
His chosen ones with a joyful shout.
He gave them also the lands of the nations,
That they might take possession
of the fruit of the peoples' labor,
So that they might keep His statutes,
And observe His laws,
Praise the Lord! (vv. 42-45).

God remembered His promise to Abraham and gave the Israelites the land of Canaan under the leadership of Joshua (c. 1490-1480 B.C.), which they occupied in part until 605 B.C. The writer of this psalm no doubt intended to remind the people of Israel that God does not forget His promises. This is in stark contrast to Psalm 78, which portrayed the history of Israel through her failures.

PSALM 106

This is another untitled psalm. As was recorded in Psalm 105, this is a companion historical psalm. Both give a poetic summary of Israel's history. These are also companion psalms in that 105 drew verses from David's song of 1 Chronicles 16. This psalm also uses verses from that same song. Some commentators believe that this one was written during the Captivity to give a different tone to the history. Leupold[12] points out that Psalm 105 is a cheery and sunny account, while Psalm 106 is somber and sad. Both are legitimate ways of looking at the facts.

Praise the Lord!
Oh give thanks to the Lord,
for He is good;
For His lovingkindness is everlasting.
Who can speak of the mighty deeds
of the Lord,
Or can show forth all His praise?
How blessed are those who keep justice,
Who practice righteousness
at all times! (vv. 1-3).

Verse 1 of this psalm is identical to 1 Chronicles 16:34, which is a song given by David to Asaph. This song may point to the possibility of the same author, although there is a distinct difference in tone between the two. Verse 2 poses the question of who can fully declare the praises of God. In verse 3 a blessing is pronounced on those who practice righteousness.

Remember me, O Lord,
in Thy favor toward Thy people;

Visit me with Thy salvation,
That I may see the prosperity of Thy chosen ones,
That I may rejoice in the gladness of Thy nation,
That I may glory with Thine inheritance (vv. 4, 5).

The writer pleads to be remembered when God favors Israel. Is he suggesting that he is not an Israelite by birth? Probably not, but he may be suggesting that he is not automatically worthy to receive their blessings for reasons not revealed.

We have sinned like our fathers,
We have committed iniquity, we have behaved wickedly.
Our fathers in Egypt did not understand Thy wonders;
They did not remember Thine abundant kindnesses,
But rebelled by the sea, at the Red Sea.
Nevertheless He saved them for the sake of His name,
That He might make His power known.
Thus He rebuked the Red Sea and it dried up;
And He led them through the deeps, as through the wilderness.
So He saved them from the hand of the one who hated them,
And redeemed them from

the hand of the enemy.
And the waters covered their adversaries;
Not one of them was left.
Then they believed His words;
They sang His praise (vv. 6–12).

The confession of national sin begins in verse 6, where the psalmist pleads that his forefathers did not understand God's way. They rebelled at the sea but God saved them, while their adversaries were drowned. Then they believed God and sang His praises.

They quickly forgot His works;
They did not wait for His counsel,
But craved intensely in the wilderness,
And tempted God in the desert.
So he gave them their request,
But sent a wasting
disease among them (vv. 13-15).

The people of Israel again forgot God's goodness. In the desert (c. 1485-1445 B.C.) they tested God concerning their food. God sent them meat in abundance, but along with it, He sent disease that killed many among them.

When they became envious
of Moses in the camp,
And of Aaron, the holy one of the Lord,
The earth opened and swallowed up Dathan,
And engulfed the company of Abiram.
And a fire blazed up in their company;
The flame consumed the wicked (vv. 16-18).

They rebelled against Moses and Aaron, whom God had chosen to lead them. Because of this, God caused the earth to open up and swallow some of the rebellious ones. He also sent fire to burn the wicked during the wilderness wanderings.

They made a calf in Horeb,
And worshiped a molten image.
Thus they exchanged their glory
For the image of an ox that eats grass.
They forgot God their Savior,
Who had done great things in Egypt,
Wonders in the land of Ham,
And awesome things by the Red Sea.
Therefore He said that He would destroy them,
Had not Moses His chosen one
stood in the breach before Him,
To turn away His wrath
from destroying them (vv. 19–23).

At Horeb (Sinai) they made a golden calf and worshiped it as a god, instead of worshiping the God of heaven. God announced to Moses that He would destroy all of them and start over, but Moses intervened and God relented.

Then they despised the pleasant land;
They did not believe His word,
But grumbled in their tents;
They did not listen to the voice of the Lord.
Therefore He swore to them
That He would cast them
down in the wilderness,
And that He would cast

their seed among the nations,
And scatter them in the lands (vv. 24-27).

Since they refused to fight for Canaan, God made them wander in the wilderness and vowed to scatter their descendants among the heathen.

They joined themselves also to Baal-peor,
And ate sacrifices offered to the dead.
Thus they provoked Him
to anger with their deeds;
And the plague broke out among them.
Then Phinehas stood up and interposed;
And so the plague was stayed.
And it was reckoned
to him for righteousness,
To all generations forever (vv. 28-31).

The Israelites made sacrifices to idols and God sent a plague that would have destroyed them all if Phinehas had not shown his trust in God (Numbers 25:7). Phinehas was a priest of the line of Aaron. Nevertheless, 24,000 were killed in the plague.

They also provoked Him to wrath
at the waters of Meribah,
So that it went hard
with Moses on their account;
Because they were rebellious
against His Spirit,
He spoke rashly with his lips (vv. 32, 33).

They rebelled against God at Meribah. In his anger, Moses struck the rock instead of speaking to it. This displeased God so that He refused Moses entrance into the Promised Land (Numbers 20:12).

They did not destroy the peoples,
As the Lord commanded them,
But they mingled with the nations,
And learned their practices,
And served their idols,
Which became a snare to them.
They even sacrificed their sons
and their daughters to the demons,
And shed innocent blood,
The blood of their sons and their daughters,
Whom they sacrificed to the idols of Canaan;
And the land was polluted with the blood.
Thus they became unclean in their practices,
And played the harlot in their deeds
(vv. 34-39).

The Israelites worshiped the idols of Canaan and sacrificed their own children to demons. Yet they expected the Lord to deliver them and protect them.

Therefore the anger of the Lord
was kindled against His people,
And He abhorred His inheritance.
Then He gave them
into the hand of the nations;
And those who hated them ruled over them.
Their enemies also oppressed them,
And they were subdued under their power.
Many times He would deliver them;
They, however, were rebellious

in their counsel,
And so sank down in their iniquity
(vv. 40-43).

Because of their disobedience, God allowed the nations to oppress them. But when God relented and blessed them, they still did not worship or serve Him.

Nevertheless He looked upon their distress,
When He heard their cry;
And He remembered His covenant
for their sake,
And relented according to
the greatness of His lovingkindness.
He also made them objects of compassion
In the presence of all their captors
(vv. 44-46).

When God heard their cry, He remembered His covenant; and because of His covenant and His love, He delivered them.

Save us, O Lord our God,
And gather us from among the nations,
To give thanks to Thy holy name,
And glory in Thy praise.
Blessed be the Lord, the God of Israel,
From everlasting even to everlasting.
And let all the people say, "Amen."
Praise the Lord! (vv. 47, 48).

The ending verses for this psalm are those taken from 1 Chronicles 16:35, 36. It is an appropriate ending for a psalm that was otherwise filled with the failure of God's people.

PSALM 137

Neither the Hebrew nor Chaldee used a title for this psalm. The Vulgate and Septuagint say it was "A Psalm of David for Jeremiah." But since it was composed during or at the close of the Captivity, neither could have had a part in it. As in some other sections, writings of both these men could have been brought into the composition. There is, however, no specific evidence of this.

By the rivers of Babylon,
There we sat down and wept,
When we remembered Zion.
Upon the willows
in the midst of it
We hung our harps.
For there our captors
demanded of us songs,
And our tormentors mirth, saying,
"Sing us one of the songs of Zion"
(vv. 1-3).

The past tense used in this section causes us to conclude that the Captivity was past. But it was also quite fresh in the mind of the writer. The opening verse indicates the love for the Holy City the captives brought with them.

The Jews would naturally gather by the river, because the presence of water helped in the ceremonial absolutions. Also, it was a partial means of escape from the eye of their captors while they began to rebuild a worship ritual. They were first planted by the River Chebar, which was really a canal constructed as a means of irrigation between the Tigris and the Euphrates Rivers. Babylon was full of such constructions because of the need to irrigate areas that would otherwise be desert.

They expressed their love not just for Jerusalem but also for the Temple, the holy services, and the godly men who served as priests of the Temple. When the oppressors called for a song to be amused by these captives, they were in no mind to oblige. This was not the atmosphere in which they had been accustomed to singing the songs of praise to God.

How can we sing the Lord's song
In a foreign land?
If I forget you, O Jerusalem,
May my right hand forget her skill.
May my tongue cleave
to the roof of my mouth,
If I do not remember you,
If I do not exalt Jerusalem
Above my chief joy (vv. 4-6).

The writer here changes from the plural past to the first person present when he makes his vow to God. He calls evil upon himself if he should forget Jerusalem. The curse seems heavy when we note in verses 5 and 6 the maledictions mentioned.

Remember, O Lord,
against the sons of Edom
The day of Jerusalem,
Who said, "Raze it, raze it,
To its very foundation."
O daughter of Babylon,
you devastated one,

How blessed will be the one
who repays you
With the recompense
with which you have repaid us.
How blessed will be the one
who seizes and dashes your little ones
Against the rock (vv. 7-9).

This section was dealt with in the imprecatory elements. God was called upon to deal with Edom and Babylon with the same measure with which they had dealt with Israel in 605-586 B.C.). Justice calls for such retribution. It is well to note that the prophet Isaiah had called for such retribution when he prophesied the treatment of God's people by Babylon:

Their little ones also
will be dashed to pieces
Before their eyes;
Their houses will be plundered
And their wives ravished.
Behold, I am going to stir up
the Medes against them,
Who will not value silver
or take pleasure in gold,
And their bows will
mow down the young men,
They will not even have compassion
on the fruit of the womb,
Nor will their eye pity children.
And Babylon, the beauty of kingdoms,
the glory of the Chaldeans' pride,

Will be as when God overthrew
Sodom and Gomorrah (Isaiah 13:16-19).

The destruction of Babylon as prophesied by Isaiah occurred c. 520 B.C.

9

Hallelujah Psalms

The last five psalms of the book (146-150) are known as the Hallelujah Psalms because the beginning and ending words are "Praise the Lord"—a translation of the Hebrew words *Hallelu Yah.* This is really a compound word—*Hallelu,* meaning "praise," and the Hebrew *Yah,* meaning "Lord."

We sometimes see this word translated *Alleluia,* which is a Greek modification of the word *Hallelujah.* The important thing is that the reader understands that none of these change the meaning of the term. All of these mean "Praise the Lord."

We also need to distinguish these from the Hallel Psalms (113-118), dealt with elsewhere. There are many other psalms containing the term *Hallelujah,* but in the Hallelujah Psalms this word in the Hebrew is found both at the beginning and ending of the five psalms. There is a specific reason for this grouping. The 150 psalms are divided with the praise concept.

Book 1 ends with Psalm 41:13, which reads:

Praise be to the Lord,
the God of Israel,
from everlasting to everlasting.
Amen and Amen.

Book 2 ends with Psalm 72:20. Verses 18 and 19 are praises, and verse 20 identifies this psalm as being the ending of David's writing.

Praise be to the Lord God,
the God of Israel,
who alone does marvelous deeds.
Praise be to his glorious name forever;
may the whole earth
be filled with his glory.
Amen and Amen (vv. 18, 19).

Book 3 ends with Psalm 89:52:

Praise be to the Lord forever!
Amen and Amen.

Book 4 ends with Psalm 106:48:

Praise be to the Lord,
the God of Israel,
from everlasting to everlasting.
Let all the people say, "Amen!"

Book 5 ends with the five psalms of praise—chapters 146 through 150. These represent the five books of the Psalms. What we are obviously reviewing here is the fact that these psalms were written centuries apart and gathered in books at different times (see reference to close of 2nd book). It is believed that an unknown writer united these psalms in order to have songbooks for the new Temple after the return from captivity.

What does this have to do with the Hallelujah Psalms? A great deal. There are five such songs. The writer wanted to represent each book with a full psalm of praise, so he wrote a psalm and began it with "Praise the Lord," and ended it the same way to represent a praise for the first four. To close the entire five books, he composed a song in which every verse contained a praise to the Lord and ended it with a final "hallelujah," or "Praise the Lord," as he had each of the books.

In the introduction I mentioned that this person was probably Ezra, although none of these songs are titled. These last five were certainly in the Ezra-Nehemiah period, which was a part of the Persian period that began in 450 B.C. and continued to 330 B.C. Scholars are divided on Ezra and Nehemiah, but we know that Ezra led a revival after the return and the second Temple was built. What greater thing could he do than to pull together the scrolls with Israel's history, which was also a history of God's deliverance? The last five songs (146-150) are believed to have had a special place in the ceremony at the new Temple, according to tradition of the Talmud (see ch. 1).

Psalm 146

None of the five Hallelujah Psalms carry titles or authors. But it is possible to estimate the date of this psalm. Leupold[1] says it is a comparatively late date—probably in the time of Haggai or Zechariah. On this there is no unanimity of thought. Most scholars believe the entire group to be postexilic.

Praise the Lord.
Praise the Lord,
O my soul.
I will praise the Lord
all my life;
I will sing praise to my God
as long as I live (vv. 1, 2).

The writer first invites all who read to praise the Lord. Then he exhorts his own soul to praise God. He follows with the determination to praise God as long as he lives. Nothing could stop his praises.

Do not put your trust in princes,
in mortal men,
who cannot save (v. 3).

He exhorts everyone to put no trust in earthly leaders. The term *princes* refers to leaders who can make decisions as they please. They are mere men who go back to the earth, as do other men when they die. When they die all their promises are without effect. Some read into this a time period when the edict of Cyrus had been suspended and work on rebuilding the Temple had to be stopped. The Samaritans were doing all they could to influence the Persian government not to renew aid to the Jews. If the assumption is true, this helps date the psalm (c. 536 B.C.).

Blessed is he whose help is the God of Jacob,
whose hope is in the Lord his God,
the Maker of heaven and earth,

the sea, and everything in them—
the Lord, who remains
faithful forever (vv. 5, 6).

Notice that the psalmist refers to the God of Jacob, rather than the God of Israel. After the 10 tribes broke away, they were known as Israel and the southern tribes as Judah. The choice of Jacob predated that time and covers both north and south. In spite of their captivity, he speaks of a God who "remains faithful forever." Only the restoration from captivity could bring such a strong response.

He upholds the cause of the oppressed
and gives food to the hungry.
The Lord sets prisoners free,
the Lord gives sight to the blind,
the Lord lifts up those
who are bowed down,
the Lord loves the righteous (vv. 7, 8).

Upholding the cause of the oppressed may again refer to their release from Babylon, just as the phrase "sets prisoners free" may include that action. The picture of the Lord's lifting up those who are "bowed down" could also represent the release. He could now say, "The Lord loves the righteous." During captivity there were many psalms of distress.

The Lord watches over the alien
and sustains the fatherless and the widow,
but he frustrates the ways of the wicked (v. 9).

"The Lord watches over the alien"—they had been aliens in Babylon. The psalmist does not forget to mention the fatherless and the widows, as God had constantly exhorted them to do, but he notes that God "frustrates the ways of the wicked." Those who had overrun Jerusalem were themselves taken captive, and so the way of the wicked was frustrated.

The Lord reigns forever,
your God, O Zion,
for all generations.
Praise the Lord (v. 10).

Their God was still a just God; this is the God of Zion, which again suggests they are back and secure in their homeland. Praise the Lord (Hallelujah)!

Psalm 147

As are the other Hallelujah Psalms, this one is untitled and its date is post-Captivity. In this psalm the Jews were rebuilding Jerusalem, and the song is a praise to God for the safety of the walls and the joy of construction of the city (c. 520-516 B.C.). It should be observed that the Septuagint divides this work into two psalms (vv. 1-11, 12-20). This would seem to make the Septuagint list one more psalm than the Hebrew version, but another change keeps this from happening. The Septuagint combines Psalms 9 and 10 into one, so the Hebrew and the Greek versions retain the 150 psalms (Delitzsch[2]).

Praise the Lord.
How good it is
to sing praises to our God,
how pleasant and fitting
to praise him!
The Lord builds up Jerusalem;
he gathers the exiles of Israel.

He heals the brokenhearted
and binds up their wounds (147:1-3).

Praise God! The walls around Jerusalem have been constructed again and safety has been provided for its inhabitants. The historical setting is described in Nehemiah 12:27-43. The term *build up* means of course "to rebuild." The gathering of exiles comes not only from the return from Babylon. As the city was built up (c. 444 B.C.), other Jews who were scattered abroad made their way back to Zion. The phrase "exiles of Israel" would suggest that some of the pious from the northern kingdom found their way back to the center of their heritage. The emotional and spiritual recovery is identified in verse 3 by the healing of the brokenhearted and the binding up of wounds.

In order to bring the restoration into focus historically, Delitzsch[3] describes a helpful sequence. In the seventh year of Artaxerxes I, Ezra returned to Jerusalem with about 2,000 exiles, most of whom were Levites (458 B.C.). Thirteen years later (445 B.C.) Nehemiah, who had been the personal servant to the king, returned with the express purpose of rebuilding the walls and gates of the city so that future building projects could be protected. This allowed Ezra, the priest, to give himself to the spiritual restoration of the people. It was during this restoration, many scholars believe, that Ezra gathered the scrolls that contained the songs and poems of God's people and placed the five books into a single book. He probably also added these five Hallelujah Psalms and wrote an introduction to Psalms, the song which became Psalm 1.

He determines the number of the stars
and calls them each by name (v. 4).

In verse 4, the writer turns from praising God for deliverance and restoration to praising Him for maintaining the universe. It should not seem strange that the God who created the stars should assign names to them and know how many there are. If He could call this planet Earth, it is not difficult to identify the millions of heavenly bodies He created.

Verse 5 emphasizes the fact that there is no limit to God's understanding. Everything we do not understand, He fully understands. That is why when we take a problem to Him, we do not have to plan the solution. He already knows what should be done.

Verse 6 underscores what we learned in Psalm 1. There are only two kinds of people—the righteous and the wicked. Here, God is seen strengthening the righteous, but casting out the wicked.

> *Sing to the Lord with thanksgiving;*
> *make music to our God on the harp.*
> *He covers the sky with clouds;*
> *he supplies the earth with rain*
> *and makes grass grow on the hills.*
> *He provides food for the cattle*
> *and for the young ravens*
> *when they call* (vv. 7–9).

In verse 7 the psalmist introduces stringed instruments into the worship of God—praising Him on the harp for all His goodness. In verse 8 he shows the connection and sequence of God's activity in the weather. He does not see weather as a happenstance, but as a direct act of God. The land of Palestine is a dry country, but God calls the clouds to supply rain. The rain brings grass to the hills for the benefit of cattle and the lowly raven and ultimately for the good of mankind.

His pleasure is not in the strength of the horse,
nor his delight in the legs of a man;
the Lord delights in those who fear him,
who put their hope
in his unfailing love (vv. 10, 11).

God is not awed by the strength of a horse because He made him capable of carrying burdens and pulling heavy loads. The swiftness of the runner in battle is a gift from God. But there is something in which He takes delight: those who reverence Him and who put their hope in His unfailing love. The righteous can hope in His mercy regardless of the circumstance in which they find themselves.

Extol the Lord, O Jerusalem;
praise your God, O Zion,
for he strengthens the bars of your gates
and blesses your people within you.
He grants peace to your borders
and satisfies you
with the finest of wheat (vv. 12–14).

Praise God! He has strengthened the security of the walls and gates of Jerusalem. What was once torn down is now rebuilt. God is worthy to be praised. The security thus attained blesses the people with protection that they had hereto not enjoyed. They are now strong enough to protect themselves from those around them, and God has supplied them with food in abundance.

He sends his command to the earth;
his word runs swiftly.
He spreads the snow like wool
and scatters the frost like ashes.
He hurls down his hail like pebbles.
Who can withstand his icy blast?
He sends his word and melts them;
he stirs up his breezes,
and the waters flow (vv. 15–18).

His word is the basis for the changing patterns in the earth, including the elements. Ice and snow are quite unusual in the Holy Land, so the people look upon them with special awe as God's demonstration of His powers. The snow reminds them of wool and the frost of white ashes scattered over the land. The hail is hurled like pebbles and, in the history of Israel, was often used as a weapon against their enemies. They see also His power in removing these things from the earth—the ice melts, the warm breezes blow, and the water begins to flow. We understand more the science of these things than did the people of that century, but they were caught in the awe of God, which we sometimes overlook.

He has revealed his word to Jacob,
his laws and decrees to Israel.
He has done this for no other nation;
they do not know his laws (vv. 19, 20).

God has revealed His statutes to His people. No other nation has the written Word of God. What was delivered on Mount Sinai was expanded and explained by Moses in the wilderness. God continued to speak to His people through

His prophets. The contact Israel had with the people of Babylon proved to them that they had a Word superior to any other nation. This was ample reason to praise the Lord.

Psalm 148

There is no reason to question that this psalm, as well as the other Hallelujah Psalms, was written after the Jews returned to their homeland from Babylonian captivity. It is understandable that the exhortation to praise the Lord occurs at least 10 times in the 14 short verses. It occurs eight times in the first four verses:

> *Praise the Lord.*
> *Praise the Lord from the heavens,*
> *praise him in the heights above.*
> *Praise him, all his angels,*
> *praise him, all his heavenly hosts.*
> *Praise him, sun and moon,*
> *praise him, all you shining stars.*
> *Praise him, you highest heavens*
> *and you waters above the skies* (vv. 1–4).

In these psalms you hear no laments, no prayers for revenge. *Hallelujah* is the theme of all and the special word for the day and hour so far as the Jews were concerned.

It is natural that the psalmist begins with "Praise the Lord from the heavens," for there God has His throne. To praise Him "in the heights above" suggests that there are things and people whom we can only imagine from whom God should receive praise. This of course includes the angels and all His hosts of heaven. They belong to Him in the special sense of creation.

The writer then goes on to specific heavenly bodies which he can observe: "Praise him, sun and moon" (v. 3). These are the two heavenly bodies which most influence the earth—"the greater light to govern the day and the lesser light to govern the night" (Genesis 1:16). The writer also specifies the "shining stars." It is very likely he had the planets in mind. When he adds "you highest heavens," he had in mind places he could not see, perhaps the heaven where God is, in contrast to the heaven of the stars and the lower heavens where the birds fly.

Let them praise the name of the Lord,
for he commanded and they were created.
He set them in place for ever and ever;
he gave a decree
that will never pass away (vv. 5, 6).

At His command, all things that were created came into being. This is reason enough for God to receive glory from them. He spoke and they were created (Genesis 1). God gave them being, and His divine power keeps them in place "for ever and ever." This would be what we usually call the forces of nature. In reality, there are no forces of nature that operate apart from God.

Praise the Lord from the earth,
you great sea creatures
and all ocean depths,
lightning and hail,
snow and clouds,
stormy winds that do his bidding (vv. 7, 8).

Next, the writer urges all sea creatures to praise the Lord. This would include the whale, the sharks, porpoises and sea monsters that dwell in the lowest parts of the sea. Whereas he began with the highest heavens, the writer now visits the deepest valleys of the sea and calls on all who live there to praise the Lord. He then goes to the intermediate area in which storms with lightning, thunder, wind, hail, snow, sleet and all kinds of natural occurrences do His bidding.

> *You mountains and all hills,*
> *fruit trees and all cedars* (v. 9).

What about the living beings on the earth? Let them all praise God! Hallelujah! All that live in the high mountains, the goats that live among high rocks, the precious stones in the rocks, the minerals under the mountains—all were called forth by His word and are commanded to respond with "Praise the Lord."

We are not to forget the trees that bear fruit for men's benefit. Unto God they bear fruit—the Georgia peach, the bountiful banana bunches, the Washington apples, the delicious pecans. Their fruit is their way of saying "Praise the Lord." Also the nonfruit-bearing trees—the cedars of Lebanon from which David built his palace, the sturdy oaks that house millions of families inside their constructed form, and the evergreens that men bring into their homes at Christmastime—all give glory to God by serving His people.

> *Wild animals and all cattle,*
> *small creatures and flying birds* (v. 10).

The writer does not forget the animals. The wild deer and antelope, the bear and the elephant, the wolf and the lion—all have a place in God's economy and their existence praises God. He does not forget the domesticated cattle, the chicken and the duck, the horse and the cow. Even the smallest creatures, such as the squirrel and rabbit, furnish both food and fur for the highest of God's creation. Verse 10 also includes the sparrow who builds her nest in the yard tree, and the robin who announces spring with his red breast and song of joy. Hallelujah!

Kings of the earth and all nations,
you princes and all rulers on earth,
young men and maidens,
old men and children (vv. 11, 12).

Kings who rule the earth under God's authority should praise Him. Old men walking on crooked sticks and children playing catch should praise Him. The young men in their prime and the maidens in their beauty all are called to give praise to the God of all creation.

Let them praise the name of the Lord,
for his name alone is exalted;
his splendor is above
the earth and the heavens.
He has raised up
for his people a horn,
the praise of all his saints,
of Israel,
the people close to his heart.
Praise the Lord (vv. 13, 14).

Let all these, and those not mentioned, praise the eternal God who sustains all and supports all! God has exalted the horn of His people and extended His mercies to all. Israel had been brought out of Babylon—surely she cannot forget to shout, "Hallelujah!"

This restoration is no accident. God planned and foretold it by His prophets. He brought it to pass by King Cyrus, who did not know Israel's God. But God used Cyrus for this purpose so he should deliver Israel. Hallelujah! Praise the Lord!

PSALM 149

An excellent introduction to this psalm is given by Delitzsch[4]. He affirms that the author of both Psalms 148 and 149 is the same and supports the argument with internal evidence. He believes the war drums are the result of the strengthened self-consciousness of the period after Cyrus. The time may be about the time of Esther, when she persuaded the king of Persia to allow the Jews to defend themselves with swords if their enemies came within their homes. Although this incident took place in Persia, among Jews who did not return to their homeland, it would have greatly influenced those now in Jerusalem to know that the king had believed Queen Esther and armed the Jews (c. 473 B.C.).

At the same time, Delitzsch insists that the Christian church cannot pray as the Old Testament church prays here. It was this psalm that the Roman Catholic princes used for support when they fought a bloody 30-year war (Ellicott, p. 299). Also, he attributes the War of the Peasants by the Protestants, led by Thomas Monzen (1618-1648), to this same psalm. He warns them that the Christian church must remember that "the weapons of our warfare are not carnal" (2 Corinthians 10:4, KJV).

Praise the Lord.
Sing to the Lord a new song,

his praise in the assembly of the saints.
Let Israel rejoice in their Maker;
let the people of Zion be glad in their King.
Let them praise his name with dancing
and make music to him
with tambourine and harp.
For the Lord takes delight in his people;
he crowns the humble
with salvation (vv. 1–4).

"Sing to the Lord a new song." It was new in that it was not the song of captivity and defeat—it was a song of victory and gladness. The song of Israel was no longer a lament for the loss of Jerusalem but now a "Praise God" for restoration. Israel now rejoiced in Him who made them, and praise was heard in the assembly of the saints. The people of Zion rejoiced in their King and no nation asked, "Where is their God that He does not deliver them?" There could be no doubt now that God rejoiced in His people and that He would deliver them. He would save those who had been humbled. For this reason, they danced and made music to Him with the tambourine and harp. The Jews were often demonstrative in their worship, especially in times of great victory.

Let the saints rejoice in this honor
and sing for joy on their beds.
May the praise of God be in their mouths
and a double-edged sword in their hands,
to inflict vengeance on the nations
and punishment on the peoples,
to bind their kings with fetters,
their nobles with shackles of iron,

to carry out the sentence written against them.
This is the glory of all his saints.
Praise the Lord (vv. 5–9).

This rejoicing was not to be limited to the public worship. It continued at home on their beds. It is to be a lifelong attitude of the child of God so delivered. The song of the Lord was to be on their lips and the sword of the Lord in their hands. Thus would they carry out God's command to destroy the heathen. Verse 9 indicates that this is no wild bloodthirsty party—it is a divine energy to carry out what God has determined against His enemies. The glory of His people is to carry out His will. Praise the Lord!

Psalm 150

This final Hallelujah psalm is also the close of the entire book. Each of the five books of Psalms closes with "Praise the Lord." This psalm is intended to close the entire book in like manner. The word *praise* occurs 13 times in this short psalm of six verses.

Delitzsch[5] points out that the Jews see in their synagogue 13 divine attributes. He assumes there is a deliberate correspondence. The grand finale seems to use all the instruments the Hebrews attached to praise. It is a musical display performed with a full orchestra and choir—with wind instruments, stringed instruments and percussion—and then all who have breath are invited to join in (Ellicott[6]).

Praise the Lord.
Praise God in his sanctuary;
praise him in his mighty heavens.
Praise him for his acts of power;

praise him for his surpassing greatness.
Praise him with the sounding of the trumpet,
praise him with the harp and lyre,
praise him with tambourine and dancing,
praise him with the strings and flute,
praise him with the clash of cymbals,
praise him with resounding cymbals.
Let everything that has breath
praise the Lord.
Praise the Lord (vv. 1–6).

Hallelujah! "Praise God in his sanctuary," which some see not in the Temple in Jerusalem, but in His heavenly dwelling place. All creation is invited to praise Him in His "mighty heavens."

If verse 1 tells who is to be praised, verse 2 continues by telling us why He is to be praised:

- For His acts of power, including His creation; and for the Hebrews, a long list of deliverances—from Egypt, in the land of Canaan, in the rebuilding of the city of Jerusalem and the Temple, where He was pleased to dwell.
- For His personal greatness.

After praising Him for *who* He is and *why* we should praise Him, the writer turns to *how* we should praise Him. He is to be praised with the sound of the *trumpet,* the clear sound that calls His people to assembly. Also with the *harp* (a stringed instrument), which was the favorite instrument of young David in the field, as well as King David in the palace. The *lyre* (Hebrew, *nebel*) was a hollow stringed instrument perhaps much like the guitar of modern times. Praise Him with the *tambourine,* which is still popular in some areas; praise Him with *dance*. Clarke[7] thinks the word never meant dance as we understand it, but it referred to the pipe (*machol*). Delitzsch[8], however, sees no problem in the festive dance that was often accompanied by the tambourine. Praise is also to be offered by the *strings* in their most encompassing meaning and the *flute* that was a shepherd's pipe.

Verse 5 continues with explaining the how—by the clash of *cymbals*. There seems to have been two types of cymbals—a smaller clear-sounding instrument often called the "high-sounding cymbal" and the deep-toned cymbal, which was louder. In 1 Chronicles 15:19, Heman, Asaph and Ethan were to play the bronze cymbals, suggesting there may have been a variety of metals used for the difference in sound. No one offers a description of the "resounding" cymbal. It is possible that it was loud enough to reverberate, but it may be a term without specific meaning except the ability to make a loud noise.

Having told us who was to be worshiped, why He was to be worshiped, and how He was to be worshiped, the psalmist closes with exhortation as to who was to be involved—everything that has breath is to praise the Lord. Hallelujah!

Messianic Prophecies

The Book of Psalms is not a book of prophecy. When we think of the prophetic books in the Old Testament, we think of the Major and Minor Prophets written by men called to give forth the word of the Lord which included both forthtelling and foretelling. Generally we attach the prophetic title to one that has been called of God to deliver His word to His people.

The function of the prophet can best be understood by the terms used to describe his role—*seer* (*ro'eh*) and *spokesman* (*nab'i*) in the Hebrew. The English word *prophet* is from the Greek word *prophetes*, which means "one who speaks for another."[1] Although the Book of Psalms is filled with prophetic passages, the speaker is not thought to be like those in the Prophetic Books. Rather, in Psalms we find the prophetic element bursting forth in the midst of worship, thanksgiving and sorrow. Sometimes these words are words of God's message of deliverance and encouragement; sometimes they are expressions of His displeasure. In either case, little is made of the spokesman as is done in the Prophetic Books. Rather, the Holy Spirit injects God's message in such a way that even the speaker may not be aware of the new message that has been revealed.

Here in Psalms, as elsewhere, prophecy may have a double sense. In the case of Isaiah, the prophet declared that "a virgin [Hebrew, *almah*] will be with child and bear a son, and she will call His name Immanuel" (Isaiah 7:14). This prophecy was concerning the Messiah who would redeem Israel, but in the short term it was a reassurance to the king of Israel that the people of God would not be destroyed in battle. It seemed at that time they would fall to Syria.[2] So the prophecy, which would be fulfilled almost 800 years later, was also assurance of immediate victory. Without the immediate deliverance, there would be no future Messiah of the house of David. So it is in Psalms that a prophecy may have a double meaning with the distant truth not revealed at that time.

We also need to distinguish between those psalms that are messianic in their primary meaning, and those that contain a messianic element. "Many psalms, written a thousand years before Christ, contain references to Christ that are wholly inapplicable to any other person in history."[3] Some seem to be referring to a king that would come from David's family; others are a foreshadowing of the Messiah. We will begin by dealing first with those psalms that are historically accepted as messianic and then look at those elements which seem to foreshadow the coming King.

SECTION ONE
MESSIANIC PSALMS

Psalm 2

This is the first of the Messianic Psalms. Like Psalm 1, this one does not have a title. Just as the first psalm was an introduction to the book, there are some who believe that both Psalms 1 and 2 are introductions, since all other psalms in books 1 and 2 are titled. If this is true, Psalm 1 would be an introductory psalm setting forth the nature of man as being either wicked or righteous, while Psalm 2 would be a continuation of this theme showing that the wicked nations would be broken under the rod of God's Son, who was to come.

Why are the nations in an uproar,
And the peoples devising a vain thing?
The kings of the earth take their stand,
And the rulers take counsel together
Against the Lord and
against His Anointed (vv. 1, 2).

According to the Book of Acts, these two verses had been fulfilled, and the writer attributed them as having been spoken by the Holy Ghost through the mouth of David.

"Who by the Holy Spirit,
through the mouth of our father
David Thy servant, didst say,
Why did the Gentiles rage,
And the peoples devise futile things?
'The kings of the earth took their stand,

And the rulers were gathered together
Against the Lord,
and against His Christ'" (Acts 4:25, 26).

This would indicate that the hostility of the Jews and the Gentiles against Jesus was being foretold in the first two verses of Psalm 2. This relationship was not accidental. It was a plan executed with the cunning knowledge of both. At the time of Christ, the Jewish nations had no power to put any man to death because they were under Roman control. But there is no doubt that the leaders of Israel connived to deliver Christ to the Gentiles, who placed Him on the cross.

"Let us tear their fetters apart,
And cast away their cords from us!"
He who sits in the heavens laughs,
The Lord scoffs at them.
Then He will speak to them in His anger
And terrify them in His fury:
"But as for Me, I have installed
My King upon Zion,
My holy mountain" (Psalm 2:3-6).

Verse 3 expresses the determination of the world not to be brought into bondage to God's precepts. Just as the Sinai words were thrown off, even so now the wicked would break the last hold that heaven had placed on the earth. Man would easily accept the God of the universe if He would throw off all restraints upon man.

But God scoffs at such an idea. God has His plan and man will follow it or be broken on the decision to reject the Savior of the world, whom God prepared before the foundations of the earth. Now He reveals that the gospel will first be preached on Zion and from there it will go to all the ends of the earth. The King has been chosen, and the world (including Israel) will either accept Him or suffer the consequence.

> *"I will surely tell of the decree of the Lord:*
> *He said to Me, 'Thou art My Son,*
> *Today I have begotten Thee.*
> *'Ask of Me,*
> *and I will surely give the nations*
> *as Thine inheritance,*
> *And the very ends of the earth*
> *as Thy possession.*
> *'Thou shalt break them*
> *with a rod of iron,*
> *Thou shalt shatter them*
> *like earthenware'"* (vv. 7-9).

Verse 7 has to do with the proclamation that Christ is the Son of God. The word *Christ* (Greek, *Christos*) is the equivalent to the Hebrew term *Messiah*. The Son would declare the eternal purpose of God—that the believer would be redeemed by Christ's blood and sanctified by the Spirit. His death would prove that the Atonement had been made. The Resurrection would prove that the Atonement had been accepted. These were the words of the Son. Verse 8 is the response of the Father, because by the Resurrection, He had been declared the Son of God. And the purpose of God was that in Him would dwell all the fullness of the Godhead bodily.

> *"And we preach to you the good news*
> *of the promise made to the fathers,*

that God has fulfilled this promise
to our children
in that He raised up Jesus,
as it is also written
in the second Psalm,
'Thou art My Son;
today I have begotten Thee'"
(Acts 13:32, 33).

Again we see this truth reflected in the Book of Hebrews:

For to which of the angels did He ever say,
"Thou art my Son,
Today I have begotten Thee"? (1:5).

Hebrews calls a third scripture into witness:

And no one takes the honor to himself,
but receives it when he is called by God,
even as Aaron was.
So also Christ did not glorify Himself
so as to become a high priest,
but He who said to Him,
"Thou art My Son,
Today I have begotten Thee" (5:4, 5).

In the final three verses of this psalm, we find an exhortation for reconciliation with the Son:

Now therefore, O kings, show discernment;
Take warning, O judges of the earth.
Worship the Lord with reverence,
And rejoice with trembling.
Do homage to the Son, lest He become angry,

and you perish in the way,
For His wrath may soon be kindled.
How blessed are all
who take refuge in Him! (Psalm 2:10-12).

This exhortation is for the rulers of the earth to receive the Son as they would the law of the land. The Lord is to be feared as a sovereign king receives obedience from a servant. Those who truly serve God cannot help but be happy. All such joy must be based on the obedience rendered to the Sovereign King. The word *Son* here is the Chaldee *bar* and is a strange selection in a Hebrew passage where the word *Son* would have been *ben.* It was probably chosen from the Chaldee, rather than the Hebrew, for a reason that is not clearly understood by the scholars.

Since all judgment was given to the Son, the world leaders are admonished to show signs of friendship, as bestowing a kiss would have been in the Oriental countries of that day. It must note here that good must eventually triumph over evil, and all who do not submit themselves will be filled with great fear and trembling.

Psalm 8

Psalm 8 is ascribed to David with the musical instruction "on the Gittith." A Talmudic paraphrase is "on the kinnor which was brought from Gath." This would make it a Philistine flute.[4] The term would have no relation to the subject matter of the psalm, since the word also appears in Psalms 81 and 84. Delitzsch[5] observes that the psalm was probably written at night, since verse 3 calls attention to the moon and stars but makes no mention of the sun. What we do know about its theme from the internal evidence is that it speaks of the mystery of the universe and reflects the theme of Genesis 1. Without the messianic element, it might simply be a song about the mystery of the universe.

But because of this element, Halley[6] gives it the title "Man through Messiah to become Lord of Creation."

O Lord, our Lord, How majestic is
Thy name in all the earth,
Who hast displayed Thy splendor
above the heavens!
From the mouth of infants and nursing babes
Thou hast established strength,
Because of thine adversaries,
To make the enemy and the revengeful
cease (vv. 1, 2).

Jesus quoted verse 2 to explain to His disciples an incident in His own ministry.

"Do You hear what these are saying?"
And Jesus said to them,
"Yes; have you never read,
'Out of the mouth of infants
and nursing babes
Thou hast prepared praise for Thyself'?"
(Matthew 21:16).

This not only indicates that the Book of Psalms is full of references to Christ, but that Christ was also a man of the Psalms. What was in the mind of David when he lifted his eyes into the heavens and talked about infants and children? Surely only the Holy Spirit could have authored such a thought.

When I consider Thy heavens,
the work of Thy fingers,
The moon and the stars,
which Thou hast ordained;
What is man,
that Thou dost take thought of him?
And the son of man,
that Thou dost care for him?
Yet Thou hast made him
a little lower than God,
And dost crown him
with glory and majesty!
Thou dost make him to rule
over the works of Thy hands;
Thou hast put all things under his feet,
All sheep and oxen,
And also the beasts of the field,
The birds of the heavens,
and the fish of the sea,
Whatever passes through
the paths of the seas.
O Lord, our Lord,
How majestic is Thy name
in all the earth! (8:3-9).

The writer of Hebrews did not hesitate to find Christ in this picture. It was so familiar to him that he did not even bother to find the reference.

For He did not subject to angels
the world to come,
concerning which we are speaking.
But one has testified somewhere,

saying, "What is man
that Thou rememberest him?
Or the son of man,
that Thou art concerned about him?
"Thou hast made him for a little while
lower than the angels;
Thou hast crowned him
with glory and honor,
And hast appointed him
over the works of Thy hands;
Thou hast put all things in subjection
under his feet" (Hebrews 2:5-8).

He may not have given a reference because this same truth appears in another place in Scripture. The reading is slightly different, but the truth is the same.

O Lord, what is man,
that Thou dost take knowledge of him?
Or the son of man,
that Thou dost think of him? (Psalm 144:3).

Who has not looked into the starry skies and thought, as David did, of what the Lord had in mind when He created such a limitless panorama of beauty? But only by the Holy Spirit could David have spoken of the Christ-to-be. No doubt David thought of man's weakness and insignificance as he looked into the skies. But the Holy Spirit caused him to speak of One who would come from man and who would rule the world for God's glory. He would be born into the family of man, a little under the angels, and raised to the place of dominion and glory for which man was originally created.

Psalm 16

The title of this psalm says that it is a *mikhtam* of David. This term is sometimes spelled as *michtam* and means "a golden poem."[7] It is also found in the titles of five other psalms by David (Psalms 56-60). It is indeed a "golden poem," because in it we find pictured the resurrection of the Messiah.

Preserve me, O God,
for I take refuge in Thee.
I said to the Lord,
"Thou art my Lord;
I have no good besides Thee" (vv. 1, 2).

David was great because he always recognized the greatness of God and his own unworthiness as expressed here.

As for the saints who are in the earth,
They are the majestic ones
in whom is all my delight (v. 3).

David finds nothing good apart from God, but he quickly recognizes the good in others. How uncharacteristic this is of most of us, who see our own virtues but are quick to recognize the vices of others.

The sorrows of those
who have bartered for another god
will be multiplied;
I shall not pour out their libations of blood,
Nor shall I take their names upon my lips (v. 4).

Here David makes the division that is made in Psalm 1, and a theme that is carried throughout the entire book—man is either godly or wicked. The psalmist not only praises the godly, but he also affirms that he will in no wise be identified with the wicked. In verse 4 he emphasizes the most wicked of all—the idolaters.

The Lord is the portion of my inheritance
and my cup;
Thou dost support my lot.
The lines have fallen to me
in pleasant places;
Indeed, my heritage is beautiful to me
(vv. 5, 6).

David was happy with the lot God had assigned him. How unlike many of us who say to God, "Oh, if only I had the chances You have given to others." God is his portion and he is satisfied with his present and future in Him.

I will bless the Lord
who has counseled me;
Indeed, my mind instructs me
in the night (v. 7).

David is happy with the way God has led him. Even at night when he thinks upon his decision to go God's way, he is convinced that he has made the right choice.

I have set the Lord continually before me;
Because He is at my right hand,
I will not be shaken (v. 8).

His future is secure because he has placed it in God's hands.

Therefore my heart is glad,
and my glory rejoices;

My flesh also will dwell securely.
For Thou wilt not abandon
my soul to Sheol;
Neither wilt Thou allow Thy Holy One
to undergo decay.
Thou wilt make known to me
the path of life;
In Thy presence is fulness of joy;
In Thy right hand
there are pleasures forever (vv. 9-11).

The apostle Peter brings these statements into New Testament focus when he states:

"For David says of Him,
'I was always beholding the Lord
in my presence;
For He is at my right hand,
that I may not be shaken.
'Therefore my heart was glad
and my tongue exulted;
Moreover my flesh also
will abide in hope;
Because Thou wilt not abandon
my soul to Hades,
Nor allow Thy Holy One
to undergo decay'" (Acts 2:25-27).

The words of David were further explained by Peter:

"Brethren, I may confidently say to you
regarding the patriarch David
that he both died and was buried,

and his tomb is with us to this day.
And so, because he was a prophet . . .
he looked ahead
and spoke of the resurrection of the Christ,
that He was neither abandoned to Hades,
nor did His flesh suffer decay" (vv. 29-31).

The Holy Spirit placed words in the mouth of the prophet, David, that he did not understand. Later it would be revealed to believers when the doctrine of the Resurrection was ready to be explained.

PSALM 22

Although this is a psalm of David, it is often called "A psalm of the Crucifixion" because its opening words are those used by Christ on the cross.

My God, my God,
why hast Thou forsaken me?
Far from my deliverance
are the words of my groaning (v. 1).

Matthew quoted these words from the mouth of Jesus at the Crucifixion scene:

And about the ninth hour
Jesus cried out with a loud voice,
saying, "Eli, Eli, lama sabachthani?"
that is, "My God, my God,
why hast Thou forsaken Me?" (27:46).

His cry indicates that He suffered separation from God for paying for the sins of a lost world. The words He used were not Hebrew, as we might suppose—they were Aramaic. After the Babylonian Captivity, the Jews spoke mostly Aramaic. Many of those about Him did not understand the words because they thought He was calling for Elijah (Matthew 27:47). Since the Old Testament was written primarily in Hebrew, the Old Testament had to be translated and explained when it was being quoted. Those who did not know what Christ was saying included the Greek-speaking Romans and those Hebrews who did not speak Aramaic. There may have been those who were out of hearing range and did not hear correctly what was spoken.

O my God, I cry by day,
but Thou dost not answer;
And by night,
but I have no rest (Psalm 22:2).

This is the lament of David, who cries out for the Lord to hear him in the time of dire distress. We do not know the historical setting with certainty, but many have concluded that it was at the time David was trying to escape from his enemy, Saul. God had not answered his prayer, just as He did not answer Jesus' cry from the cross. He had other plans. If God had spared His Son on the cross, He could not have spared those who would be saved through Him. God has reasons for delaying our prayers when we think He has forsaken us.

Yet Thou art holy,
O Thou who art enthroned
upon the praises of Israel.
In Thee our fathers trusted;

They trusted,
and Thou didst deliver them.
To Thee they cried out,
and were delivered;
In Thee they trusted,
and were not disappointed (vv. 3-5).

This was a reasonable argument for David. If God answered prayer in the past, why should He not answer now? There is a sense in which Jesus laid claim to the entire psalm when He quoted the opening lines. This same reasoning could have been His. We are not to think that Jesus knew all the time why God was not answering. This was no game that the Messiah was playing out. This was true distress in which the Son, at that moment, did not know what the Father was doing because it had not been revealed to Him by the Spirit.

But I am a worm,
and not a man,
A reproach of men,
and despised by the people (v. 6).

Jesus was being treated in a most brutal manner. He did not imagine that men despised Him. Even his nation, Israel, had delivered Him to the Roman authorities for crucifixion.

All who see me sneer at me;
They separate with the lip,
they wag the head, saying,
"Commit yourself to the Lord;
let Him deliver him;
Let Him rescue him,
because He delights in him" (vv. 7, 8).

Matthew caught the emotion of the crowd in chapter 27:

And those passing by
were hurling abuse at Him,
wagging their heads, and saying,
"You who are going to destroy the temple
and rebuild it in three days,
save Yourself!
If You are the Son of God,
come down from the cross."
In the same way the chief priests also,
along with the scribes and elders,
were mocking Him, and saying,
"He saved others;
He cannot save Himself.
He is the King of Israel;
let Him now come down from the cross,
and we shall believe in Him.
He trusts in God;
let Him deliver Him now,
if He takes pleasure in Him;
for He said,
'I am the Son of God'" (vv. 39-43).

It is difficult to determine what separates David's feeling of rejection from those experienced by Christ.

Yet Thou art He who didst
bring me forth from the womb;
Thou didst make me trust
when upon my mother's breasts.
Upon Thee I was cast from birth;
Thou hast been my God

from my mother's womb
Be not far from me,
for trouble is near;
For there is none to help (Psalm 22:9-11).

This was not a happenstance that such words would be used in reference to our Savior. Isaiah later gave us the same picture:

He was despised and forsaken of men,
A man of sorrows,
and acquainted with grief;
And like one
from whom men hide their face,
He was despised,
and we did not esteem Him (53:3).

Note also the picture of men as animals crying out against Him:

Many bulls have surrounded me;
Strong bulls of Bashan have encircled me.
They open wide their mouth at me,
As a ravening and a roaring lion
(Psalm 22:12, 13).

The bulls of Bashan are described the largest and most fierce animals that grew up on the rich meadows north of Jabbok, known as the land of Og, before it came to be the land of Manasseh (Numbers 32:33).

I am poured out like water,
And all my bones are out of joint;
My heart is like wax;

It is melted within me.
My strength is dried up like a potsherd,
and my tongue cleaves to my jaws;
And Thou dost lay me
in the dust of death (Psalm 22:14, 15).

A potsherd was a piece of pottery (usually in a broken state) that had been cast away. God, it seemed, had cast him aside as useless. At that moment, that was the human view.

For dogs have surrounded me;
A band of evildoers has encompassed me;
They pierced my hands and my feet (v. 16).

Thomas refused to believe unless he saw what was prophesied in Psalm 22 and what he had seen with his own eyes while Jesus was on the cross.

The other disciples therefore
were saying to him,
"We have seen the Lord!"
But he said to them,
"Unless I shall see in His hands
the imprint of the nails,
and put my finger into the place of the nails,
and put my hand into His side,
I will not believe" (John 20:25).

Thomas was an eyewitness and had seen His horrible death. There is no doubt about what he saw according to the testimony of John.

I can count all my bones.
They look, they stare at me;

They divide my garments among them,
And for my clothing
they cast lots (Psalm 22:17, 18).

Matthew also testifies the following:

And when they had crucified Him,
they divided up His garments
among themselves,
casting lots (27:35).

The Christ of the cross begins to pray to Him who was able to deliver:

But Thou, O Lord, be not far off;
O Thou my help, hasten to my assistance.
Deliver my soul from the sword,
My only life from the power of the dog.
Save me from the lion's mouth;
And from the horns of the wild oxen
Thou dost answer me (Psalm 22:19-21).

When all else failed, the Messiah still made His prayer to God. It is difficult for us to understand God turning His back without explaining to His Son why. But the sacrifice and the turning away had to be real in order for the payment of sin to be made.

I will tell of Thy name to my brethren;
In the midst of the assembly
I will praise Thee.
You who fear the Lord, praise Him;
All you descendants of Jacob, glorify Him,
And stand in awe of Him,

all you descendants of Israel.
For He has not despised
nor abhorred the affliction of the afflicted;
Neither has He hidden His face from him;
But when he cried to Him for help,
He heard (vv. 22-24).

The writer of Hebrews calls attention to the fact that Jesus is not ashamed to call them (those who are sanctified) brothers, as He says:

"I will proclaim Thy name to My brethren,
In the midst of the congregation
I will sing Thy praise" (2:12).

Here we clearly see the prophecy that the Messiah will be resurrected. How could He otherwise declare God's name among the brethren? We also learn that God has heard the cry of His Son and will deliver Him after the Atonement is finished.

From Thee comes my praise
in the great assembly;
I shall pay my vows
before those who fear Him.
The afflicted shall eat and be satisfied;
Those who seek Him will praise the Lord.
Let your heart live forever!
All the ends of the earth will remember
and turn to the Lord,
And all the families of the nations
will worship before Thee.
For the kingdom is the Lord's
And He rules over the nations (Psalm 22:25–28).

In these verses we learn that it is in the great assembly that the vows would be fulfilled and when the Jew and the Gentile believer would meet together. Also, it states that all the families of the nations will worship the Lord.

All the prosperous of the earth
will eat and worship,
All those who go down to the dust
will bow before Him,
Even he who cannot keep his soul alive.
Posterity will serve Him;
It will be told of the Lord
to the coming generation.
They will come and
will declare His righteousness
To a people who will be born,
that he has performed it (vv. 29-31).

It isn't over until God says it is over. All who die will bow before Him, and His righteousness will be proclaimed to those yet unborn. The gospel will be preached to the heathen, and they will turn from their idols and worship Him. Both the rich and the poor shall make up His kingdom.

Psalm 110

This psalm is attributed to David. It is supported by the New Testament, as will be revealed in the discussion of the messianic prophecy in it.

The Lord says to my Lord:
"Sit at My right hand,
Until I make Thine enemies
a footstool for Thy feet" (v. 1).

When Jesus asked the Pharisees what they thought about Christ, they answered that He was the son of David.

He said to them, "Then how does David
in the Spirit call Him 'Lord,' saying,
'The Lord said to my Lord,
"Sit at My right hand,
Until I put Thine enemies
beneath Thy feet"'?" (Matthew 22:43, 44).

We learn from this passage that Jesus supported the Davidic authorship of Psalm 110. We also hear Jesus emphasize that He spoke by the Spirit when He uttered these words. We also learn that this psalm speaks of the Messiah. Look now at the Book of Acts, where we find this verse quoted on the Day of Pentecost. (This same passage is also recorded in Mark 12:36; Luke 20:42, 43.)

"For it was not David
who ascended into heaven,
but he himself says:
'The Lord said to my Lord,
"Sit at My right hand,
Until I make Thine enemies
a footstool for Thy feet."'
"Therefore let all the house of Israel
know for certain
that God has made Him
both Lord and Christ—
this Jesus whom you crucified"
(Acts 2:34-36).

We follow this psalm further to see the description of the victory promised to the Messiah over His enemies.

The Lord will stretch forth
Thy strong scepter from Zion, saying,
"Rule in the midst of Thine enemies."
Thy people will volunteer freely
in the day of Thy power;
In holy array,
from the womb of the dawn,
Thy youth art to Thee
as the dew (Psalm 110:2, 3).

This psalm is quoted more frequently in the New Testament than any other.[8] This section describes primarily the destruction of His enemies and His reign on the earth. His priesthood is confirmed in the next verse, but there is not much information describing His priestly ministry.

The Lord has sworn
and will not change His mind,
"Thou art a priest forever
According to the order
of Melchizedek" (v. 4).

The writer of Hebrews echoed these words, along with a prophecy from Psalm 2:7.

So also Christ did not glorify Himself
so as to become a high priest,
but He who said to Him,
"Thou art My Son,
Today I have begotten Thee";
just as He says also in another passage,
"Thou art a priest forever
According to the order
of Melchizedek" (Hebrews 5:5, 6).

In the next verses the prophet David speaks of Christ's return to the earth, not as a priest, but as a warrior to defeat the earth that has long been in revolt.

The Lord is at Thy right hand;
He will shatter kings
in the day of His wrath.
He will judge among the nations,
He will fill them with corpses,
He will shatter the chief men
over a broad country.
He will drink from the brook
by the wayside;
Therefore He will lift up His head
(Psalm 110:5-7).

Some think that the shortness of this psalm means that we have only a fragment of the original. We cannot speculate on that because we have no evidence to support it. The Bible addresses this passage in the Book of Revelation.

And I saw heaven opened;
and behold, a white horse,
and He who sat upon it
is called Faithful and True;
and in righteousness He judges and wages war.
And His eyes are a flame of fire,
and upon His head are many diadems;
and He has a name written upon Him
which no one knows except Himself.
And He is clothed with a robe
dipped in blood;
and His name is called The Word of God.

And the armies which are in heaven,
clothed in fine linen, white and clean,
were following Him on white horses.
And from His mouth comes a sharp sword,
so that with it He may smite the nations;
and He will rule them with a rod of iron;
and He treads the wine press
of the fierce wrath of God, the Almighty.
And on His robe and on His thigh
He has a name written,
"KING OF KINGS, AND LORD OF LORDS"
(19:11-16).

Then the writer of Revelation describes the battle which takes place on the great and terrible day of His wrath.

And I saw the beast
and the kings of the earth
and their armies, assembled
to make war against Him
who sat upon the horse,
and against His army.
And the beast was seized,
and with him the false prophet
who performed the signs
in his presence,
by which he deceived
those who had received
the mark of the beast
and those who worshiped his image;
these two were thrown alive
into the lake of fire

which burns with brimstone.
And the rest were killed
with the sword
which came from the mouth
of Him who sat upon the horse,
and all the birds
were filled with their flesh (vv. 19-21).

Perhaps the Lord simply waited for the Book of Revelation to give a more complete picture.

SECTION TWO MESSIANIC ELEMENTS IN THE PSALMS

There are other psalms that have specific elements of prophecy concerning the Messiah. We will identify those passages in addition to the chapters just discussed.

PSALM 40

Sacrifice and meal offering
Thou hast not desired;
My ears Thou hast opened;
Burnt offering and sin offering
Thou hast not required.
Then I said, "Behold, I come;
In the scroll of the book
it is written of me;
I delight to do Thy will, O my God;
Thy Law is within my heart" (vv. 6-8).

The ears that were opened indicates the servitude of Christ to the will of God. The writer of Hebrews makes it plain that the body of the Messiah was to do what the body of animals could not do:

Therefore, when He comes
into the world, He says,
"Sacrifice and offering
Thou hast not desired,
But a body
Thou hast prepared for Me;
In whole burnt offerings
and sacrifices for sin
Thou hast taken no pleasure.
"Then I said: 'Behold, I have come
(In the roll of the book
it is written of Me)
To do Thy will, O God'" (10:5-7).

Psalm 41

Even my close friend,
in whom I trusted,
Who ate my bread,
Has lifted up
his heel against me (v. 9).

Christ applied this statement directly to Himself when He predicted His betrayal in John:

"I do not speak of all of you.
I know the ones I have chosen;
but it is that the Scripture
may be fulfilled,

'He who eats My bread
has lifted up his heel against Me'" (13:18).

Psalm 45

Thy throne, O God, is forever and ever;
A scepter of uprightness
is the scepter
of Thy kingdom (v. 6).

The New Testament speaks from this scripture:

But of the Son He says,
"Thy throne, O God,
is forever and ever,
And the righteous scepter
is the scepter of His kingdom" (Hebrews 1:8).

Psalm 69

Those who hate me without a cause
are more than the hairs of my head;
Those who would destroy me are powerful,
What I did not steal,
I then have to restore (v. 4).

Note the New Testament parallel:

"But now they have both seen and hated
Me and My Father as well.
"But they have done this
in order that the word may be fulfilled
that is written in their Law,
'They hated Me
without a cause'" (John 15:24b, 25).

This seems to be written especially to the Jews because of the reference to "their Law."

I have become estranged
from my brothers,
And an alien
to my mother's sons.
For zeal for Thy house
has consumed me,
And the reproaches
of those who reproach Thee
have fallen on me (Psalm 69:8, 9).

Note the careful mention of "my mother's sons." His disciples remembered that it was written, "Zeal for Thy house will consume me" (John 2:17). Not all the verses of Psalm 69 apply to the Messiah, but there is no question that many do.

They also gave me
gall for my food,
And for my thirst
they gave me vinegar to drink.
May their table before them
become a snare;
And when they are in peace,
may it become a trap.
May their eyes grow dim
so that they cannot see,
And make their loins
shake continually (vv. 21-23).

Note in the Book of Romans:

And David says,
"Let their table become
a snare and a trap,
And a stumbling block
and a retribution to them.
"Let their eyes
be darkened to see not,
And bend their backs forever" (11:9, 10).

Again, in Psalm 69, we see the words which will later be used in Acts 1:20.

May their camp be desolate;
May none dwell in their tents (v. 25).

"For it is written in the book of Psalms,
'Let his homestead be made desolate,
and let no man dwell in it'" (Acts 1:20).

Homestead here refers to the office of Judas, as we note another reference to this same historical situation:

Let his days be few;
Let another take his office.
Let his children be fatherless,
And his wife a widow (Psalm 109:8, 9).

Psalm 118

Blessed is the one who comes
in the name of the Lord;
We have blessed you
from the house of the Lord (v. 26).

Matthew applies this prophecy directly to Christ when He came into Jerusalem:

And the multitudes going before Him,
and those who followed after
were crying out, saying,
"Hosanna to the Son of David;
Blessed is He who comes
in the name of the Lord;
Hosanna in the highest!" (21:9).

The stone which the builders rejected
Has become the chief corner stone.
This is the Lord's doing;
It is marvelous in our eyes (Psalm 118:22, 23).

Jesus called the attention of His disciples to the fulfillment of this scripture.

Jesus said to them,
"Did you never read in the Scriptures,
'The stone which the builders rejected,
This became the chief corner stone;
This came about from the Lord,
And it is marvelous in our eyes'?"
(Matthew 21:42).

Have you given serious thought to how much the New Testament understanding of Jesus Christ has its basis in the Book of Psalms? The writers may not have fully understood all they wrote, but there is no doubt that the Spirit knew and placed the words in the mouth of those who could not have understood.

Endnotes

Chapter 1

[1] H.C. Leupold, *Exposition of the Psalms* (Grand Rapids: Baker, 1969) 1.

[2] F. Delitzsch, *Commentary on the Old Testament*, vol. 5, book 1 (Grand Rapids: Eerdmans, 1980) 15.

[3] Charles John Ellicott, *Ellicott's Commentary on the Whole Bible* (Grand Rapids: Zondervan) 83.

[4] Adam Clarke, *Clarke's Commentary*, vol. 3 (Nashville: Abingdon) 208.

Chapter 2

[1] F. Delitzsch, *Commentary on the Old Testament*, vol. 5, book 3 (Grand Rapids: Eerdmans, 1980) 243–245.

[2] H.C. Leupold, *Exposition of the Psalms* (Grand Rapids: Baker, 1969) 784–789.

[3] Delitzsch, 196–201.

[4] Leupold, 215–227.

[5] Delitzsch, 386–392.

Chapter 3

[1] Adam Clarke, *Clarke's Commentary*, vol. 3 (Nashville: Abingdon) 299.

[2] F. Delitzsch, *Commentary on the Old Testament*, vol. 5, book 1 (Grand Rapids: Eerdmans, 1980) 332–333.

[3] Delitzsch, vol. 5, book 2, 75.

[4] Henry H. Halley, *Halley's Bible Handbook* (Grand Rapids: Zondervan, 1965) 266.

[5] Charles John Ellicott, *Ellicott's Commentary on the Whole Bible* (Grand Rapids: Zondervan) 181.

[6] Ellicott, 181.

Chapter 4

[1] Adam Clarke, *Clarke's Commentary*, vol. 3 (Nashville: Abingdon) 407.

[2] Clarke, 437.

Chapter 5

[1] Charles John Ellicott, *Ellicott's Commentary on the Whole Bible*, vol. 4 (Grand Rapids: Zondervan) 268.

[2] F. Delitzsch, *Commentary on the Old Testament*, vol. 5, book 3 (Grand Rapids: Eerdmans, 1980) 269.

[3] Ellicott, 82.

[4] Adam Clarke, *Clarke's Commentary*, vol. 3 (Nashville: Abingdon) 632.

[5] Ellicott, 269.

[6] Clarke, 638.

[7] Henry H. Halley, *Halley's Bible Handbook* (Grand Rapids: Zondervan, 1965) 266.

[8] Clarke, 643.

[9] Ellicott, 273.

[10] Clarke, 649.

[11] Clarke, 653.

Chapter 6

[1] Henry H. Halley, *Halley's Bible Handbook* (Grand Rapids: Zondervan, 1965) 256.

[2] Adam Clarke, *Clarke's Commentary*, vol. 3 (Nashville: Abingdon) 343.

[3] Halley, 257.

[4] Charles John Ellicott, "St. Jerome," *Ellicott's Commentary on the Whole Bible*, vol. 4 (Grand Rapids: Zondervan) 141.

[5] Ellicott, *Ellicott's Commentary on the Whole Bible*, 234.

[6] Clarke, 539.

Chapter 7

[1] Adam Clarke, *Clarke's Commentary*, vol. 3 (Nashville, Abingdon) 225.

[2] Charles John Ellicott, *Ellicott's Commentary on the Whole Bible*, vol. 4 (Grand Rapids: Zondervan) 89.

[3] Henry H. Halley, *Halley's Bible Handbook* (Grand Rapids: Zondervan, 1965) 252.

[4] Clarke, 227.

[5] H.C. Leupold, *Exposition of the Psalms* (Grand Rapids: Baker, 1969) 74–75.

[6] Clarke, 358.

[7] Leupold, 344.

[8] F. Delitzsch, *Commentary on the Old Testament,* vol. 5, book 2 (Grand Rapids: Eerdmans, 1980) 151–152.

[9] Ellicott, 217.

Chapter 8

[1] Charles John Ellicott, *Ellicott's Commentary on the Whole Bible*, vol. 4 (Grand Rapids: Zondervan) 201.

[2] H.C. Leupold, *Exposition of the Psalms* (Grand Rapids: Baker, 1969) 573.

[3] Leupold, 578.

[4] Ellicott, 206.

[5] Ellicott, 208.

[6] Adam Clarke, *Clarke's Commentary*, vol. 3 (Nashville: Abingdon) 477.

[7] Leupold, 578.

[8] F. Delitzsch, *Commentary on the Old Testament*, vol. 5, book 2 (Grand Rapids: Eerdmans, 1980) 400.

[9] Leupold, 595.

[10] Clarke, 554.

[11] Henry H. Halley, *Halley's Bible Handbook* (Grand Rapids: Zondervan, 1965) 265.

[12] Leupold, 743.

Chapter 9

[1] H.C. Leupold, *Exposition of the Psalms* (Grand Rapids: Baker, 1969) 982.

[2] F. Delitzsch, *Commentary on the Old Testament*, vol. 5, book 3 (Grand Rapids: Eerdmans, 1980) 402.

[3] Delitzsch, 398.

[4] Delitzsch, 411-412.

[5] Delitzsch, 414.

[6] Charles John Ellicott, *Ellicott's Commentary on the Whole Bible*, vol. 4 (Grand Rapids: Zondervan) 300.

[7] Adam Clarke, *Clarke's Commentary*, vol. 3 (Nashville: Abingdon) 691.

[8] Delitzsch, 415.

Chapter 10

[1] Henry J. Flanders, *People of the Covenant* (New York: Oxford UP, 1988) 294.

[2] Paul Lee Tan, *The Interpretation of Prophecy* (Winona Lake, IN: BMH Books, 1974) 175–176.

[3] Henry H. Halley, *Halley's Bible Handbook* (Grand Rapids: Zondervan, 1965) 250.

[4] Charles John Ellicott, *Ellicott's Commentary on the Whole Bible*, vol. 4 (Grand Rapids: Zondervan) 96.

[5] F. Delitzsch, *Commentary on the Old Testament*, vol. 5, book 1 (Grand Rapids: Eerdmans, 1980) 148.

[6] Halley, 250.

[7] Halley, 253.

[8] H.C. Leupold, *Exposition of the Psalms* (Grand Rapids: Baker, 1969) 770.